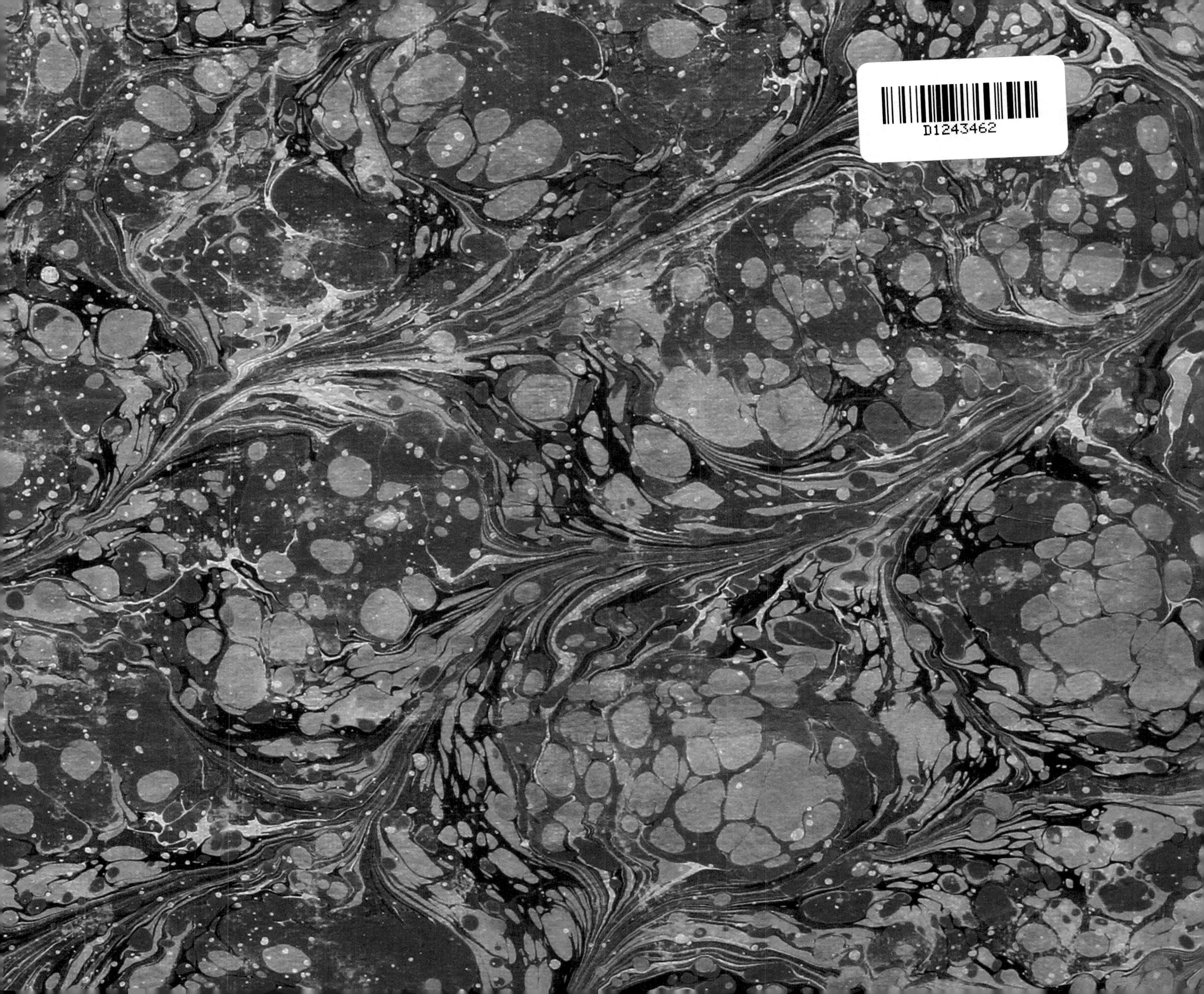
D1243462

GOLD STAMPED LEATHER TITLE OF BROWN'S BOOK
of proposals for new Castle designs and for the landscape

CAPABILITY BROWN & BELVOIR

DISCOVERING A LOST LANDSCAPE

The Duchess of Rutland
with Jane Pruden

Photography and book design by
Nick Hugh McCann
Published by Nick McCann Associates Ltd

ISBN 978-0-9516891-6-5

CAPABILITY BROWN & BELVOIR

DISCOVERING A LOST LANDSCAPE

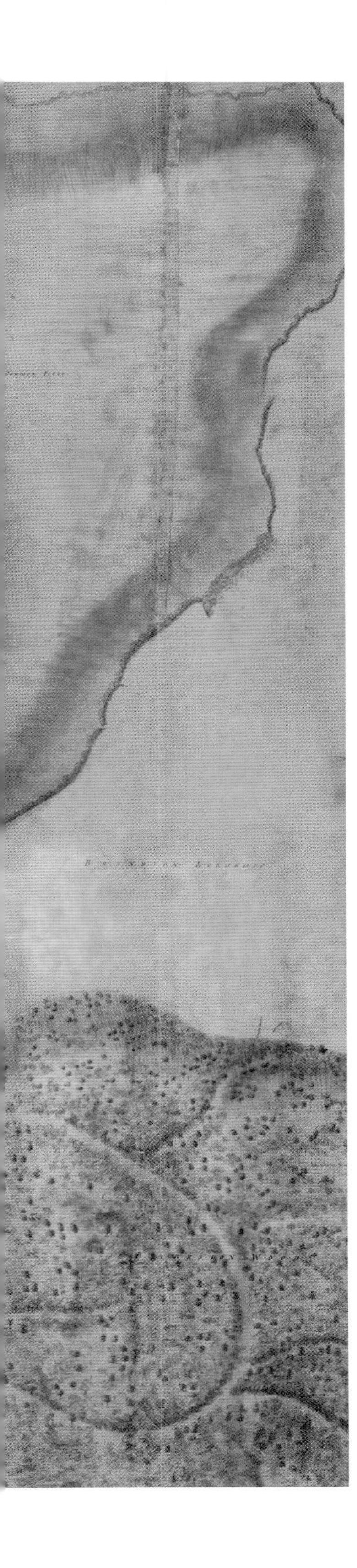

CAPABILITY BROWN drew his proposals for the Belvoir landscape twice: this large scroll for hanging on a wall and a much smaller one for the book of proposals which was easier to transport and take outside

PREVIOUS PAGE
AN EVENING VIEW OF THE CASTLE from one of Brown's viewpoints, the now demolished St. James's Church at Woolsthorpe

CONTENTS

CAPABILITY BROWN (1716 - 1783),
Sir Nathaniel Dance-Holland, Bt

Capability Brown was the most successful 18th-century landscape designer. He began working as a gardener in his native Northumberland and became William Kent's assistant at Stowe, Buckinghamshire before striking out on his own. From 1749 he worked independently, mainly as a landscape gardener. He worked for an impressive range of clients and told them that their estates had great 'capabilities'. He remoulded the parks around country houses with gentle slopes and serpentine lakes. His designs set a fashion for open, naturalistic landscapes, populated by grazing herds and punctuated by eye-catching buildings

L Brown

FOREWORD

ALAN TITCHMARSH MBE, VMH, DL

Belvoir Castle is everyone's idea of what a castle should be – an impressive stronghold sitting atop a great hill and enjoying amazing views across the Vale of Belvoir. Approach it by road and you will see it from afar – imposing, seemingly impregnable, lord of all it surveys. Home to successive Dukes of Rutland, the Castle has a colourful history, as castles tend to have, but the landscape itself also has stories to tell – especially those concerning the involvement of arguably the greatest British landscape architect of all time, Lancelot 'Capability' Brown. It was the 4th Duke of Rutland who commissioned Brown to produce a plan for the Belvoir Estate, but at the time of Brown's death the scheme remained, to Brown's great disappointment, mostly unfulfilled. A certain amount of it was implemented in the 19th century by Elizabeth, the 5th Duchess, but the majority of Brown's extensive vision was never realised. Until now.

It is to the credit of the 11th Duke and Duchess that they have decided, on the tercentenary of Lancelot Brown's birth, to implement much more of his plan – a plan that had lain buried, and generally unknown, in the Belvoir Archives until quite recently. To set eyes on it, to pore over it and see the handiwork – and handwriting – of the man himself has been a great delight, and to be asked to help in a small way to impose Brown's ideas on the 21st century landscape has been something that most folk can only dream of.

There are those who consider Brown to be a vandal – a one-trick-pony of a man who swept away all the formality of previous generations in pursuit of his own Arcadian goal. Look more closely at his career, and the development of his work, and you will see that this is far from the truth. Brown's style changed and developed over the years, and at the root of it is a degree of respect for what went before, as well as a desire to make the British landscape even more beautiful than it would be in the hands of nature alone.

The Belvoir Castle landscape is already very special; that it will finally bear something of the stamp of one of the world's finest landscape architects can only add to its glory.

ALAN TITCHMARSH

With over 40 years' experience, Alan Titchmarsh is renowned as one of the UK's top gardening experts. He is also an accomplished broadcaster and author

THE DUCHESS OF RUTLAND – EMMA
May 2015

OPPOSITE
PEN AND INK DRAWING OF BELVOIR, early 19th century, Col. Frederick Trench

INTRODUCTION

THE DUCHESS OF RUTLAND

'Brown grows very old and nothing done towards the ornament of the Castle. Since it is denied us to live long, let us do something to shew we have lived.'

Just months before he died in 1783, 'Capability' Brown, England's greatest landscape architect, wrote these poignant words in a rare letter to one of his last patrons, the 4th Duke of Rutland.

Brown's letter is just one of many astonishing documents, maps and plans that we have been discovering in our archives in a bid to learn more about our 'ornament of the castle' – the landscape gardens surrounding our family's home. Remarkably, up until now, no one really knew that much about the landscape's development, but a recent sequence of events forced us to dig deep into our family history and unearth the great mystery.

In January 2013, we had begun an extensive two-year restoration project on over 500 acres of our woodland. At the same time, we happened to be working with John Phibbs, a top surveyor and adviser for historic landscapes, who is also a leading expert on Capability Brown and instigator of the tercentenary celebrations of the latter's birth in 2016.

Quite by chance, during research for an earlier project, we had found a huge collection of plans for Belvoir that Brown had drawn up in 1780. They were checked over by garden historian, Steffie Shields and she confirmed their authenticity. The excitement was seismic because, for generations, the family believed Capability Brown had shaped the pastoral views out of every window, but we had no evidence, other than hearsay. Many of Brown's plans for his other clients had proudly hung on Estate office walls – maybe ours had too once upon a time – but for the last couple of generations, at least, they were always thought to have been lost in a devastating fire in 1816 that destroyed nearly half the Castle.

BROWN'S LETTER
to the 4th Duke of Rutland,
October 1st 1782

My Lord
To my great Mortification, on my arrival at this Place I found your Grace was gon to London. My Plan was to have paid my Duty to your Grace at Chevely to have talked over Belvoir Castle, with hopes that your Grace would have gon there as we talked when I had last the honor of seeing your Grace. I am now on my way for Lord Exeters, and Yorkshire, I should be glad to have the honor of a line from your Grace to inform me whither [whether] your Grace has any intention of being at the Castle in ten or twelve Days, whither [whether] if you have no such intention, I can be of any use on my return from Yorkshire by making Belvoir my way back. I know your Grace will adorn the Ribon[.] May your Grace be long Blessed with Health and be Ornament to your Country is the sincere wish of my Lord
Your Grace's most Obliged & Most Devoted humble Servant
Lancelot Brown

Brown grows very old and nothing done towards the ornament of the Castle. Since it is denied us to live long, let us do something to shew we have lived.

JOHN PHIBBS & EMMA survey Brown's landscape at Belvoir, winter 2014

John Phibbs is an acknowledged garden historian and specialist on the work of Capability Brown

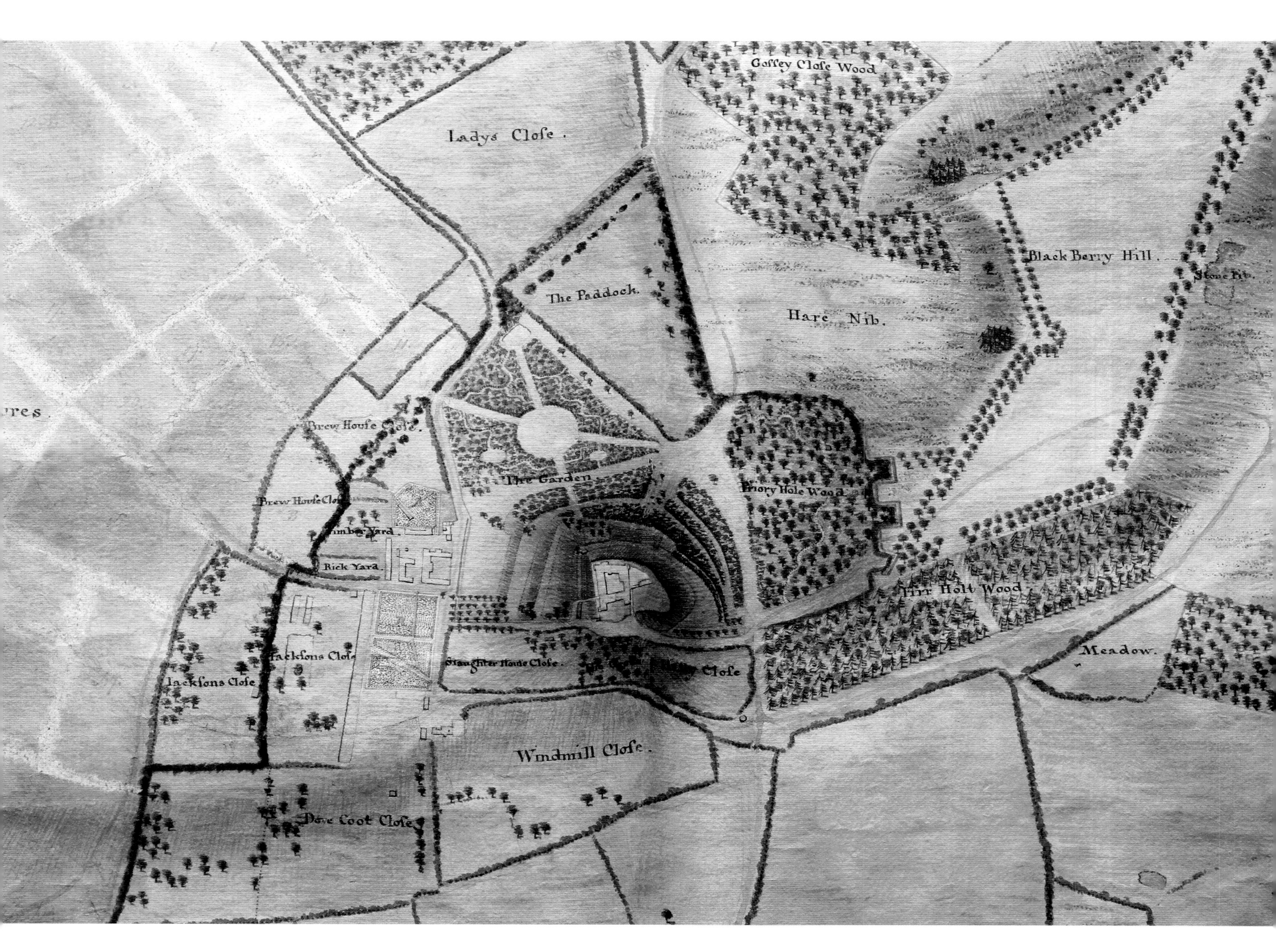

Goſſey Cloſe Wood
Ladys Cloſe.
Black Berry Hill.
Stone Pit.
The Paddock.
Hare Nib.
Brew Houſe Cloſe.
The Garden
Priory Hole Wood
Brew Houſe Cloſe
Timber Yard
Rick Yard.
Firr Holt Wood
Jacksons Cloſe
Slaughter Houſe Cloſe.
Cloſe
Meadow.
Jacksons Cloſe
Windmill Cloſe.
Dove Coot Cloſe

OPPOSITE
A DETAIL OF TOP SURVEYOR Jonathan Spyers' survey of the landscape, 1779. All the 'rubbings out' reflect the open field system once enveloped into the Enclosures

More recently still, our archivist, Peter Foden discovered a beautifully painted survey, dated 1779, by Brown's surveyor, Jonathan Spyers. Now we had some proof, and we were keen to learn more from John.

What none of us could have imagined was the impact our discoveries would have on our understanding of our landscape, and subsequent restorations. Even more pertinently, Brown's plans for Belvoir – one of his last major projects before his death – would reveal an important and significant shift in his artistic direction.

But we needed more than plans to authenticate our landscape as the work of Brown. Although the parkland certainly looks Brownian to the untrained eye with its lakes, clumps and belts of trees, and generous sweeps of verdant pasture, critics had always reminded us that it wasn't developed until the early 1800s, 20 years after Brown's death. It was widely assumed that Elizabeth, wife of the 5th Duke of Rutland, had created the parkland and lakes, as well as the formal terraces and woodland gardens in the Pleasure Grounds. It was considered to be a typical Georgian landscape of an English country seat.

PREVIOUS PAGE
VIEW TOWARDS HARSTON
from the Private Terrace

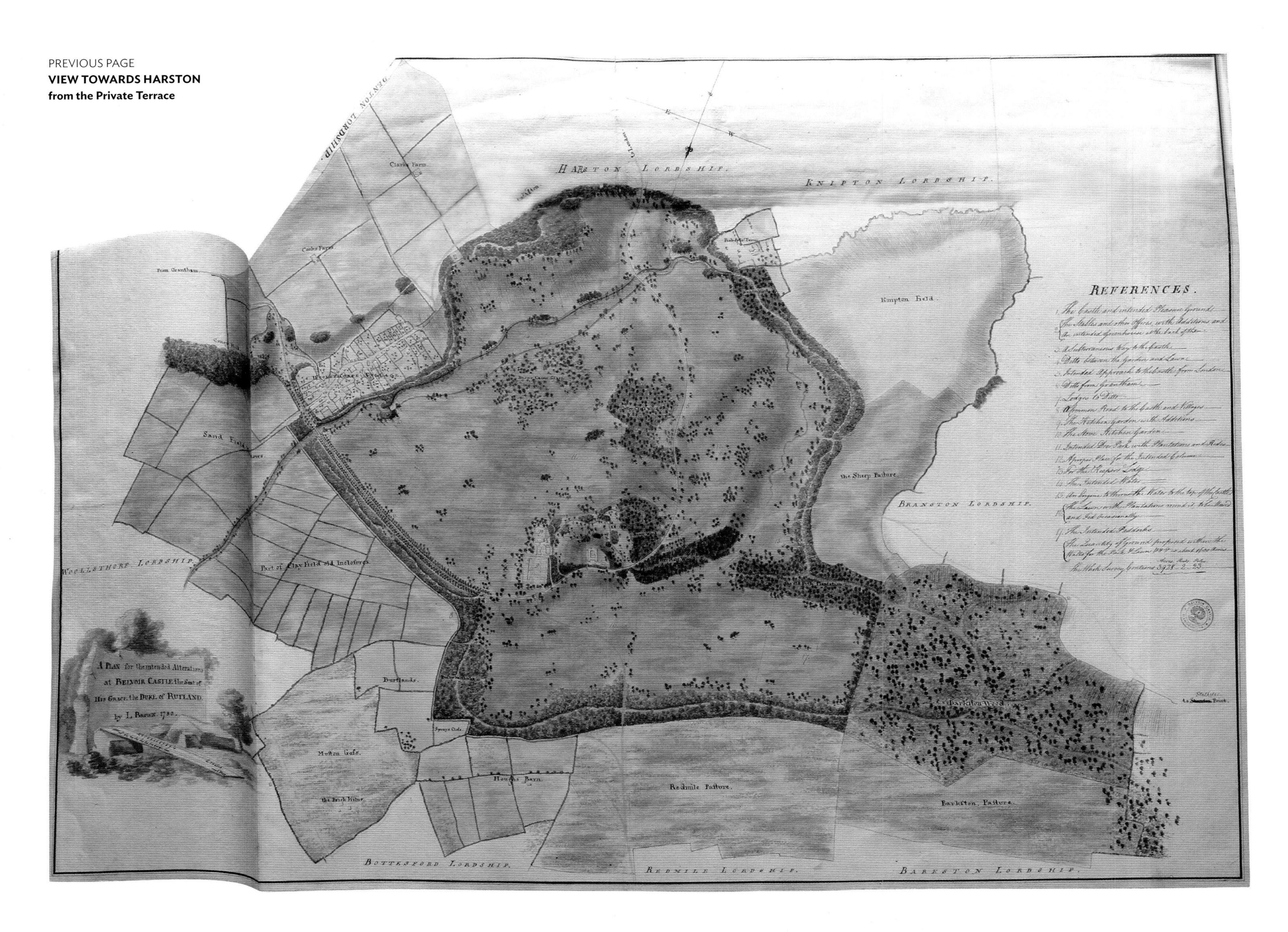

'A Plan for the intended Alterations at BELVOIR CASTLE the Seat of HIS GRACE the DUKE of RUTLAND by L BROWN, 1780', from Brown's Book of 10 proposals

OPPOSITE
A BIRD'S EYE VIEW OF THE CASTLE AND ESTATE, spring 2015, taken from the same angle as Brown's map of proposed alterations. One of the biggest differences is that the main driveway, built in the early 1800s, leads into the parkland above the village of Harston from the oak avenue on the Denton road at the top left of the picture. Brown's drive was intended further south from the village of Harston

BELVOIR CASTLE, 1814,
Thomas Wright

OPPOSITE
BELVOIR CASTLE, 200 years later in September 2014

The pretty, petite 18-year-old Lady Elizabeth Howard arrived at Belvoir in 1799 from her family home, Castle Howard in Yorkshire, to marry John, the handsome and charming 21-year-old, 5th Duke of Rutland. To say the hedonistic young bride was disappointed at the appearance of her new home and garden would be an understatement to match no other in her short life (she died aged 45, in 1825, leaving a distraught husband and seven surviving children). The Castle was no more than a squat, two-storey mid-17th-century mansion; its relatively small formal gardens had originated in the Tudor period and been added to in the 1730s. Both Castle and gardens were in a desperate state of neglect.

What does a young, rich, glamorous couple do given the opportunity to build a new home and garden? They are led by artistic fashion, which between the late 1700s and mid-1800s was driven by the Romantic Movement and advanced by informed opinion from the Grand Tour. It emerged in the wake of the libertarian and egalitarian ideals of the French Revolution and was characterised by an idealisation of nature, emotional freedom, wild imagination and humanity.

LADY ELIZABETH HOWARD
(1780-1825), John Hoppner

OPPOSITE
JOHN HENRY MANNERS,
5th DUKE OF RUTLAND
(1778-1857) c. 1794-6, John Hoppner

LEFT AND ABOVE
THE CASTLE AND LOWER LAKE
at dawn, September 2014

OPPOSITE
VIEW OF BELVOIR CASTLE,
J.M.W. Turner, 1816. The Master's work came to epitomise the Romantic Movement

Architecturally, the Romantic Movement favoured Gothic Revival. Elizabeth discounted Brown's Castle plans to create a relatively tame Gothic, neoclassical-style home and instead pushed ahead with leading Gothic romantic architect, James Wyatt, in 1801 to create a fairytale building that would reflect the prevailing Regency fashion of mediaevalism, and the Castle's genuine mediaeval history. And for the gardens, she was influenced by Picturesque, the dramatic landscaping branch of Romanticism that arose in opposition to the simplicity of Brown's smooth lines and gentle grassy countryside that rolled effortlessly into open serpentine lakes. Brown's landscapes generally looked like paintings by Claude Lorrain, whereas followers of Picturesque – generally – obsessed over the *detail* of Claude's pictures and those by Salvator Rosa. So, sublime drama in jagged rocks and rugged planting was thrown into the beautiful smooth lines of a Brownian landscape to rough it up for an alternative reading of nature.

ABOVE
LANDSCAPE, Claude Lorrain

RIGHT
BELVOIR CASTLE from the east, autumn 2014

OPPOSITE
Two of Brown's visions for the Castle, 1780

OPPOSITE
WOODED COASTAL LANDSCAPE,
attributed to Gaspard Dughet (1615-1675)

ABOVE
WOODED LANDSCAPE WITH CHRIST ON THE WAY TO EMMAUS,
Gaspard Dughet

The two inspirational paintings were most likely bought in Italy by the 3rd Duke of Rutland and would probably have been seen by Brown when he was shown round the Castle in 1780

Initially, we assumed that Elizabeth, supported by her obliging husband, had implemented Brown's plan and added her own embellishments. And yet, after months of painstaking research in our archives, we have learnt that many of the trees that Brown had proposed had already been planted and were well established by the time Elizabeth arrived. Some of the work even appears to have been carried out under his supervision. As we slowly pieced together the timeline of the garden's development, John Phibbs was also recognising a distinct new direction in Brown's thinking. Unlike his usual style, he hadn't wiped out any villages that interrupted views, nor had he swept away the existing formal gardens. His design for Belvoir also shows how much he was becoming increasingly interested in mediaeval style as a pure and English form of design by evoking the hunting scene of the Middle Ages and reinstating the warren and chase. The discoveries go some way to explaining the anachronisms in our landscape's development. But many mysteries remained, not least – why was one of Brown's most radical designs so slow to materialise from the drawing board?

We couldn't work it out. And then we discovered the full horror of the family's debts. We knew that the Castle and gardens were terribly run down and that the family was living elsewhere when Brown visited. What we didn't realise was just how close the 4th Duke was to bankruptcy. Despite commissioning the country's top landscape architect to design his garden and to remodel the Castle, the Duke's coffers were so scant that he was effectively sent away while his lawyer and agent, Joseph Hill, rescued Belvoir from penury. Hill played a hugely important role both in saving the Estate and implementing Brown's plan. Brown was a man of great vision. He didn't just transform the English countryside – he made it iconic around the world. After months of research and careful restoration, we are delighted and hugely privileged to be finally uncovering a corner of this iconic heritage on the Belvoir Estate. Many of his landscapes still surround historic country houses and, like ours, they continue to serve the same purposes for agriculture and bio-diversity, sporting and non-sporting recreation, as well as being tourist attractions.

TIMELINE SHOWING IMPORTANT FIGURES AND EVENTS OF THE 18TH CENTURY
Johann Heinrich Witschel (1769-1847)
Published by Johann Georg Klinger, Nuremberg, 1801 (engraving)

Capability Brown's importance as a world figure is highlighted in this fascinating engraving of 1801: his bust is seen 2nd from the right on the top of the design
Deutsches Historisches Museum, Berlin, Germany / © DHM / Bridgeman Images

OPPOSITE
VIEW OF BELVOIR CASTLE, 1744
Jan Griffier the Younger

OVER
VIEW OF THE CASTLE from the east on a summer evening

In 2013, we initiated a restoration programme to cover the 2,300-acres that spread out from the Castle to the perimeter tree belt because, like all landscapes, they are ephemeral and Brown's planting was choked with overgrowth in many areas. In some places we have stripped back decades of neglect to reveal many of his original views and vistas. In others, we have had the confidence to create our own adaptations of the Brownian style, and we have been able to plant – for the first time – trees on his plans that, for whatever reason, were never planted at all.

We have felled over 110 acres of woodland, planted 83,000 new trees, cleared 110 acres of overgrowth in woodland gardens, planted a new nine-acre area with a collection of unusual and rare plants that thrive on acid soil, put in 17 miles of new roads and restored 15 acres of water in long abandoned ponds and lakes. The process has not been without its fair share of disasters, steep learning curves, wonderful discoveries and an enormous sense of achievement.

But our story starts with how the landscape progressed beyond Brown's drawing board and into reality between 1779 and 1825, and the people that made it happen. Much of the work done in that period, and the projects overseen by subsequent Duchesses after Elizabeth, are reflected in my tour through the Pleasure Grounds, from the formal terraces and woodland gardens, into the parkland.

We are fortunate that Elizabeth and her husband wrote many letters about their projects at home and we have quoted from them, but sadly there is very little anecdotal material about the gardens after Elizabeth's death in 1825. Duchess Violet, wife of the 8th Duke, arrived at Belvoir as

NEW PLANTING in the Hermit's Garden, 2015; and YOUNG PLANTS in the Duchess's Garden, spring 2015 (right)

ABOVE
MAJOR REPLANTING in the woods by Old Park

BELOW
FROG HOLLOW has been cleared to reveal water features and specimen trees

chatelaine in 1906 and, as well as renovating her new home and gardens with gusto, she also wrote down many of her alterations in a notebook. Her sparse, but informative garden notes have been a priceless source of inspiration and her no-nonsense manner evokes another era. Her comments are fabulous and it's a great shame that she didn't write more. Her youngest daughter, the famous beauty Lady Diana Cooper, writes in a style that is often brisker than her mother's and we have her, and others, to thank for their hugely illuminating observations. But this is a book about Capability Brown's work at Belvoir and while – so far – we have only found one surviving letter of his to the 4th Duke, we have been blessed with a whole stash of letters in the archives sent between the 4th Duke and the redoubtable Joseph Hill. The latter's faith in Brown's plan is everywhere in our landscape and what is so interesting is that much of his advice has been paralleled in our recent restorations.

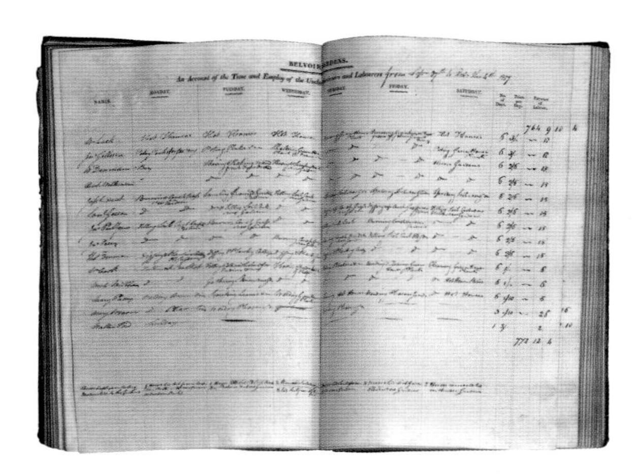

BELVOIR GARDENS,
'An Account of the Time and Employ of the Under Gardeners and Labourers from Sept 27th to Oct the 4th 1817'

Two years after the Battle of Waterloo, 14 people were employed by the 5th Duke and Duchess, with wages ranging from three shillings down to 10 pence per day. The running total for the year this week, totalled £772, 12 shillings and fourpence

LEFT
ELIZABETH 5th DUCHESS OF RUTLAND, George Sanders

OVER
A DAWN VIEW from the Castle Terrace showing Woolsthorpe Avenue to the left and (overlay), the frontispiece to Estate maps of 1799 by the 5th Duke's agent, William King

A PLAN

of LANDS in

BELVOIR

Taken in the Year

1799

CHAPTER ONE

FROM DRAWING BOARD TO REALITY
(1779 - 1825)

On an early spring day in 1780, the ageing Lancelot 'Capability' Brown would have felt every bump and pothole as his carriage clattered down the steep hill from the Great North Road into the ancient estate village of Woolsthorpe. And then his pulse must have quickened as he took in his first excited glimpse of the Duke of Rutland's family home, Belvoir Castle, perched on the opposite hilltop in its truly noble and panoramic situation. Belvoir – (pronounced beever) meaning beautiful view – would have been an irony not lost on a garden designer whose fundamental role in life was to enhance views for a living. How much gossip he had heard, or comments he may have read in contemporary literature, about the state of Belvoir at the time is impossible to know, but it is likely that this first close-up impression packed a very challenging punch. He would have seen the Castle as a distant speck 'almost in the clouds'[1] from the Great North Road (now the A1) on his many trips to work at nearby Burghley, Grimsthorpe and Stapleford Park. Perhaps he had coveted an opportunity to work at Belvoir too, but it took until almost the end of his career before the 25-year-old 4th Duke of Rutland commissioned him to draw up designs for a new Castle and garden. Brown was aged 63, and he had worked on over 250 estates before he arrived at Belvoir. Retirement, despite a lifetime suffering from asthma, constant travel and managing chaotic finances (he didn't always bill his clients), was clearly not an option.

OPPOSITE
WOOLSTHORPE AVENUE

CLOCKWISE (from above)
LADY MARY ISABELLA SOMERSET, later 4th Duchess of Rutland (1756-1831), Robert Smirke, 1799, a copy of an original portrait at Badminton House;
BELVOIR CASTLE'S north front;
CHARLES MANNERS 4th DUKE OF RUTLAND (1754-1787), Sir Joshua Reynolds;
ST. JAMES'S CHURCH, Woolsthorpe

The Duke of Beaufort, who managed the estate with his sister the Dowager Duchess Isabella until the young 5th Duke came of age, liked the look of Woolsthorpe village so much that he had a white steeple erected on the church to draw attention to it. St. James's was rebuilt in 1845 with the tower we see today

[1] Arthur Young, *A Six Months Tour through the North of England* London: W. Strachan, 1771

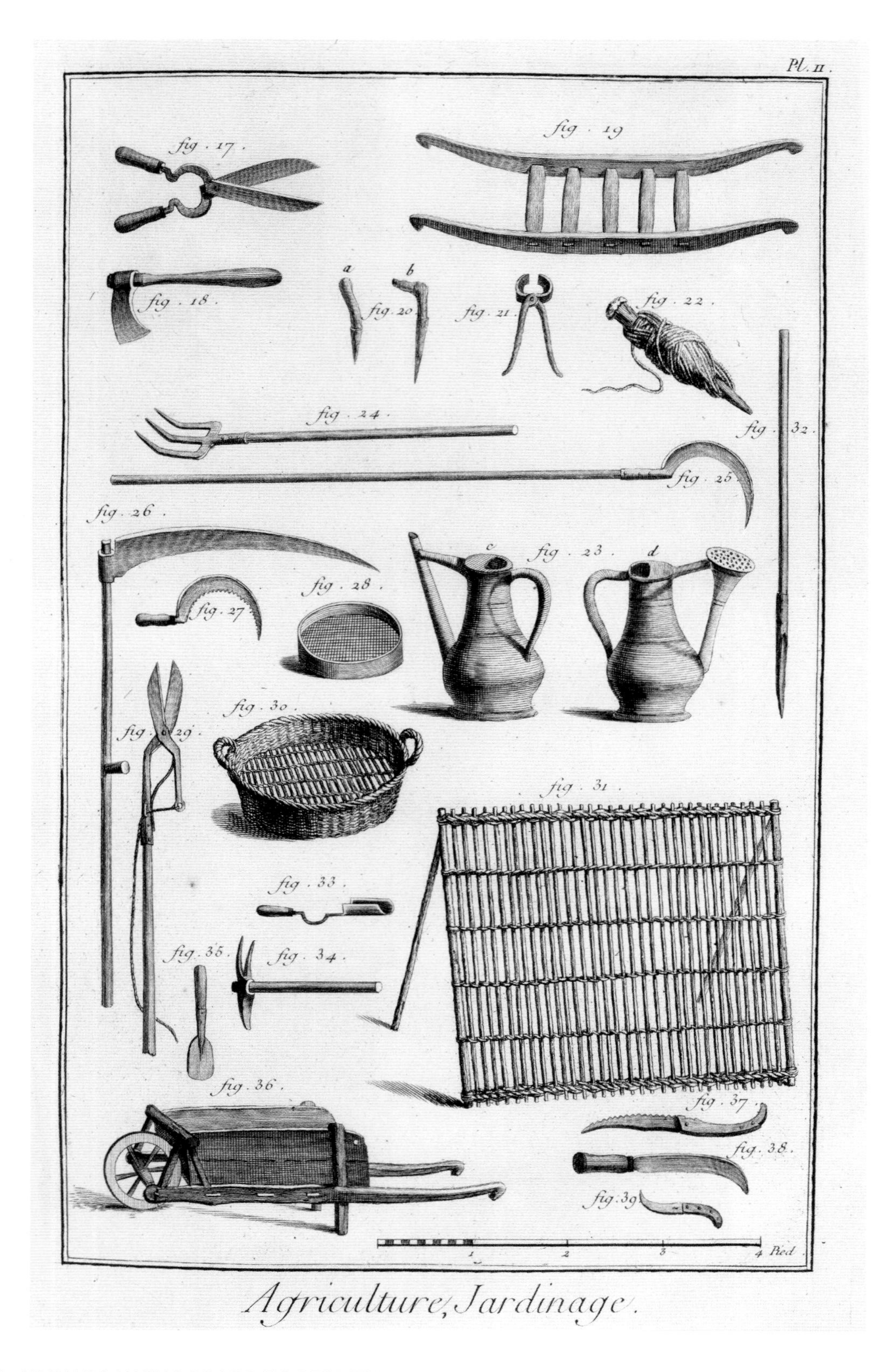

Born in 1716, in the tiny Northumbrian village of Kirkhale, surrounded by rolling green hills, Lancelot was the fifth of William and Ursula Brown's six children. Tragically, his father, who was a land agent, died in his 40s when Lancelot was four. But despite the loss, the boy grew up in a loving home with a mischievous spirit, plenty of charm[2] and a twinkle in his eye that would serve him well throughout his life. He left his village school and accepted a seven-year apprenticeship for his late father's employer, Sir William Loraine on the Kirkhale estate. He thrived. The elderly Sir William spotted young Lancelot's hard work and enthusiasm, and engaged him in his own ambitious plans for a garden that needed draining, enclosures, road building and the planting of thousands of trees.

A new style of garden was developing. The once fashionable Tudor, Dutch and French parterres were out. 'Natural' was in. By the time Brown arrived at Stowe, in 1741, to work as under gardener for William Kent he was ready to embrace the splendour of landscape style on a massive scale that would thrust his talent into the limelight. Ten years later he had moved to London with his devoted wife and family, and set up on his own.

[2] Jane Brown, *The Omnipotent Magician: Lancelot 'Capability' Brown 1716-1783*, Chatto & Windus, 2011

Brown's career as a landscape architect spanned over 50 years and he was responsible for transforming huge expanses of the British Isles and beyond into the natural Arcadian parkland that is so synonymous with English scenery. In reality, he didn't so much design a landscape as allow nature to dictate its own surroundings.

A typical design featured lakes ornamented with decorative bridges, tree clumps and pasture within a perimeter belt of trees to define the extent and status of the demesne. Grass replaced existing formal beds and parterres, often with only a ha-ha to keep out grazing sheep and cattle from the front door. His followers included King George III who appointed him as Royal Gardener at Hampton Court in 1764, as well as great landowners and writers. Horace Walpole was an enthusiast, writing: 'He sees his situation in all seasons of the year, at all times of the day. He knows where beauty will not clash with convenience, and observes in his silent walks or accidental rides a thousand hints that must escape a person who in a few days sketches out a pretty picture, but has not had leisure to examine the details and relations of every part.'[3]

[3] Horace Walpole's *Essay on Modern Gardening, 1782*

OPPOSITE
18th CENTURY GARDENING TOOLS from the *Encyclopedie des Sciences et Metiers*, Denis Diderot (1713-84) published *c.*1770 (engraving)

Private Collection / The Stapleton Collection / Bridgeman Images

LEFT (above)
JOHN MANNERS, 3rd DUKE OF RUTLAND (1696-1779), Charles Jervas. Known as 'John of the Hill'

LEFT
BRIDGET SUTTON, 3rd DUCHESS OF RUTLAND (1702-1734), (detail), Sir Godrey Kneller

His genius was matched by an easy and generous manner that allowed him to transcend all social classes. His many friends and clients came from such diverse backgrounds as the nobility and the theatre, as well as the many lawyers, agents and gardeners that he worked with over the years.

One of Brown's last commissions was to make improvements to the third Castle to stand on the Belvoir site. The first was built for Robert de Todeni, a Norman baron who had fought at the Battle of Hastings in 1066 as William the Conqueror's Standard Bearer; his Castle was the first of two to have been built as defensive strongholds. Both succumbed to the ravages of war: the Wars of the Roses and the Civil War. Two more would be built on the steep limestone ridge overlooking Leicestershire, Nottinghamshire and Lincolnshire. It was the 8th Earl and Countess of Rutland who built the third 'Castle' that Brown saw. Completed 19 years after the second Castle was destroyed on the orders of Cromwell's Parliament, in 1668, the Countess had wanted a family home with ornamental and kitchen gardens, and without any connotations of its former purpose. Her husband inherited the estates and title aged 37 through a distant cousin and reluctantly had to leave his beloved home at Haddon Hall, the family's neighbouring estate in Derbyshire. He eschewed the confrontations of the Civil War and when it was all over, and his Castle had been torn down, he had hoped to put the whole episode

LEFT (above)
THE SECOND CASTLE, tapestry by Lady Victoria Manners, early 20th century. Lady Victoria copied this from a 1632 version made by a Miss Mary Eyre

LEFT (below)
HADDON HALL, Derbyshire, John Smith

OPPOSITE (above)
THE 17th CENTURY STABLES below the castle with the circular horse walker

OPPOSITE (below left)
A MODEL OF THE CHARLES II CASTLE made in 1799 by the Revd William Mounsey, a curate at Bottesford Church.

OPPOSITE (below right)
TODAY'S CASTLE with the walls of the old kitchen garden, below right

whole episode behind him and return to life at Haddon. But his wife had other ideas and instructed John Webb, a pupil of Inigo Jones, to design plans for a palatial new residence on the Castle's old foundations. The 15th-century mediaeval towers and some of the walls of the second Castle survived into the new building. There are still some vestiges of it in the present one. Stables and a range of outbuildings were built at the same time below the northeast terrace and, apart from the 19th century covered exercise walker being added, they remain true to their original design.

Brown's journey from Woolsthorpe to the Castle would have continued its ascent along the narrow drive between hedges separating tenants' fields and over the narrow and tightly meandering River Devon, before beginning the steep climb towards the Castle walls. He would have passed the Tudor gardens – complete with canal and formal planting on the terraces – and noticed the ubiquitous wilderness, so popular in gardens of grand houses at this time. And when his driver had finally navigated his way through the mean and awkward passageway to the main entrance, Brown would have seen the 'immense prospect over a prodigiously extensive vale,'[4] and might already have had a clear idea of the capabilities in the landscape.

[4] Arthur Young, *op. cit.*

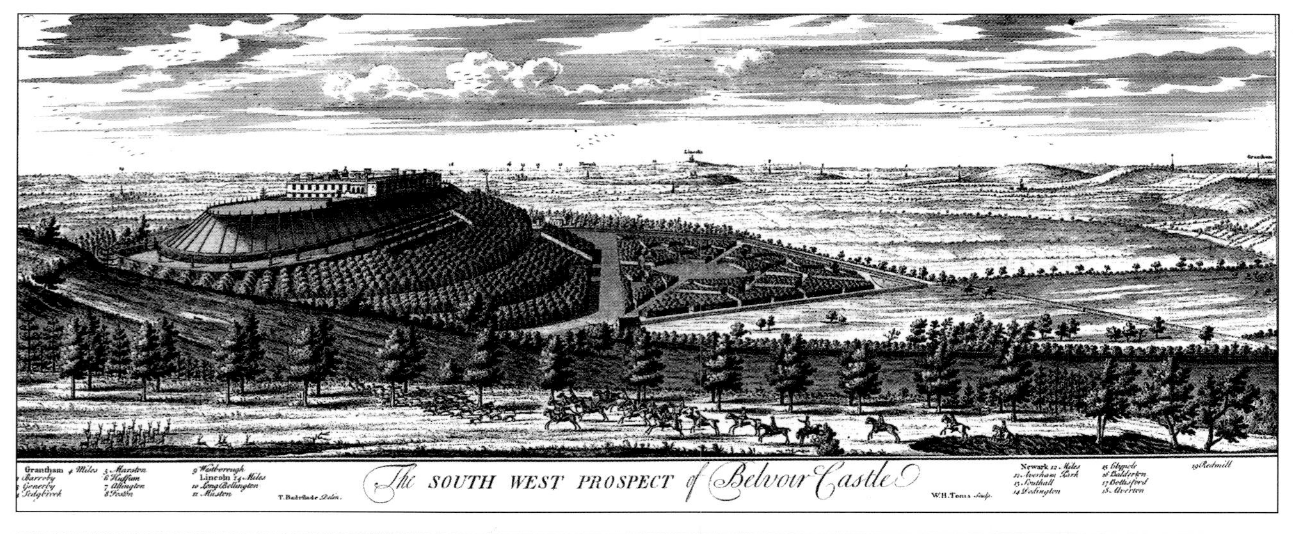

The 360° views were indeed panoramic. From the semicircular lawn on the northwest terrace, almost a *Cour d'Honneur* between stumpy projecting wings, he would have looked across the Vale to Nottingham in the far distance. From the northeast terrace, down steep formally planted terraces to the Charles II stables, was Lincoln Cathedral some 30 miles away. And across to the south, over the River Devon to Woolsthorpe, was the ruined St. James's Church – another casualty of the Civil War. The village of Knipton, or Gnipton, meaning 'the farm in the fold of the hills', lay to the southwest, before the topography swept up to the wide hilltop of Blackberry Hill ringed with an avenue of trees. The eyes then returned to the Castle over the tumbling ramparts into a steep wooded ravine and up again to the Bowling Green on the southeast terrace.

But, for all the spectacle and pomp, the Castle was shabby and shabbily run with many staff reported as being drunk and

incapable; and the landscape – poorly accessed by too few roads that were in terrible condition – was a boggy mish-mash of tenanted farms over land that wasn't all owned by the Manners family. The travel writer Arthur Young quipped in one of his books after a visit, in 1776, that: 'The house is now almost entirely unfurnished and the gardens neglected, so that it looks more like the habitation of one in distress than the seat of one of our most opulent nobles.'[5]

This was a home that had been run from a distance by an ageing grandfather, the 3rd Duke, affectionately known as 'John of the Hill'. Despite living many years in London as a widower with his mistress, Mrs Drake and his second family, he had loved Belvoir and country life; he was a conscientious and innovative landowner. But his energy for running his estates was sapped after his beloved son and heir, the great military hero, the Marquis of Granby, had died aged 49 in 1770.

OPPOSITE (above)
THE SOUTHWEST PROSPECT OF BELVOIR CASTLE, 1731

From *Vitruvius Britannicus*, J. Badeslade, J. Rocque

OPPOSITE (middle)
CASTLE VIEW OF PRESENT DAY NOTTINGHAM with the village of Redmile in the foreground

OPPOSITE (below)
A VIEW FROM THE PRIVATE TERRACES towards Knipton

LEFT
THE MARQUIS OF GRANBY (1721-1770), Sir Joshua Reynolds

[5] Arthur Young, *op. cit.*

When John died, in 1779, the Estate passed to the Marquis's eldest son, Charles. He was 25 when he became the 4th Duke and, after a childhood spent living for the most part at Cheveley Park in Newmarket, Belvoir must have felt very rundown, unloved and dated when he arrived with his beautiful wife, Mary Isabella and their three small children. So, it was quite reasonable to get the best man for the job, Capability Brown, to redesign the whole shooting match, as quickly as possible. It didn't seem to bother anyone that he couldn't afford to carry out any of the landscape designer's proposals.

As I've learnt more about our surroundings and the man who designed them, the more privileged I feel. Even after contributing designs to over 250 landscapes, it appears Brown was still working out new ideas to improve his own standards. Who could have blamed him, given his advancing years, if he had knocked out a pastiche of all the many landscapes he'd worked on before and taken the money? But, remarkably, he was still trying new things, still breaking his own traditions and still looking to improve his formula. As well as being one of his last major projects, Belvoir was his most radical landscape ever. In hindsight, the extract in his letter to the 4th Duke (see introduction), suggests not so much an eagerness for work, as an enthusiasm to create something new. But he never saw the results: a few months later, he suddenly collapsed and died outside his daughter's house in London.

One of the most significant changes for Belvoir in the 18th century had been the effect of the Enclosures, which enabled the open field systems to be acquired and brought into the private landscape. For hundreds of years, yeomen had been farming their land right up to the borders of the formal gardens of their landlords. You can still see traces of ridge and furrow in places. We know from records in our Belvoir Archives that John of the Hill had been gradually enclosing land to consolidate the Estate from 1727. Successive Dukes would continue the process to secure control, provide contiguous land for agriculture and hunting, and allow for a bigger garden. It also allowed for roads that rumbled too close to the Castle to be diverted. Belvoir's wilderness garden, planted in 1730, so curiously named by today's standards because it was a formal parterre planted with exotics, still exists. It's been overgrown for generations but its original position resulted from diverting a public road. This was because ladies would not have countenanced being overlooked by labourers during their daily constitutions.

LEFT
THE MANNERS FAMILY FLAG flies from one of the Castle turrets

OPPOSITE
WHEELBARROW, 1773 (engraving)

Private Collection / The Stapleton Collection / Bridgeman Images

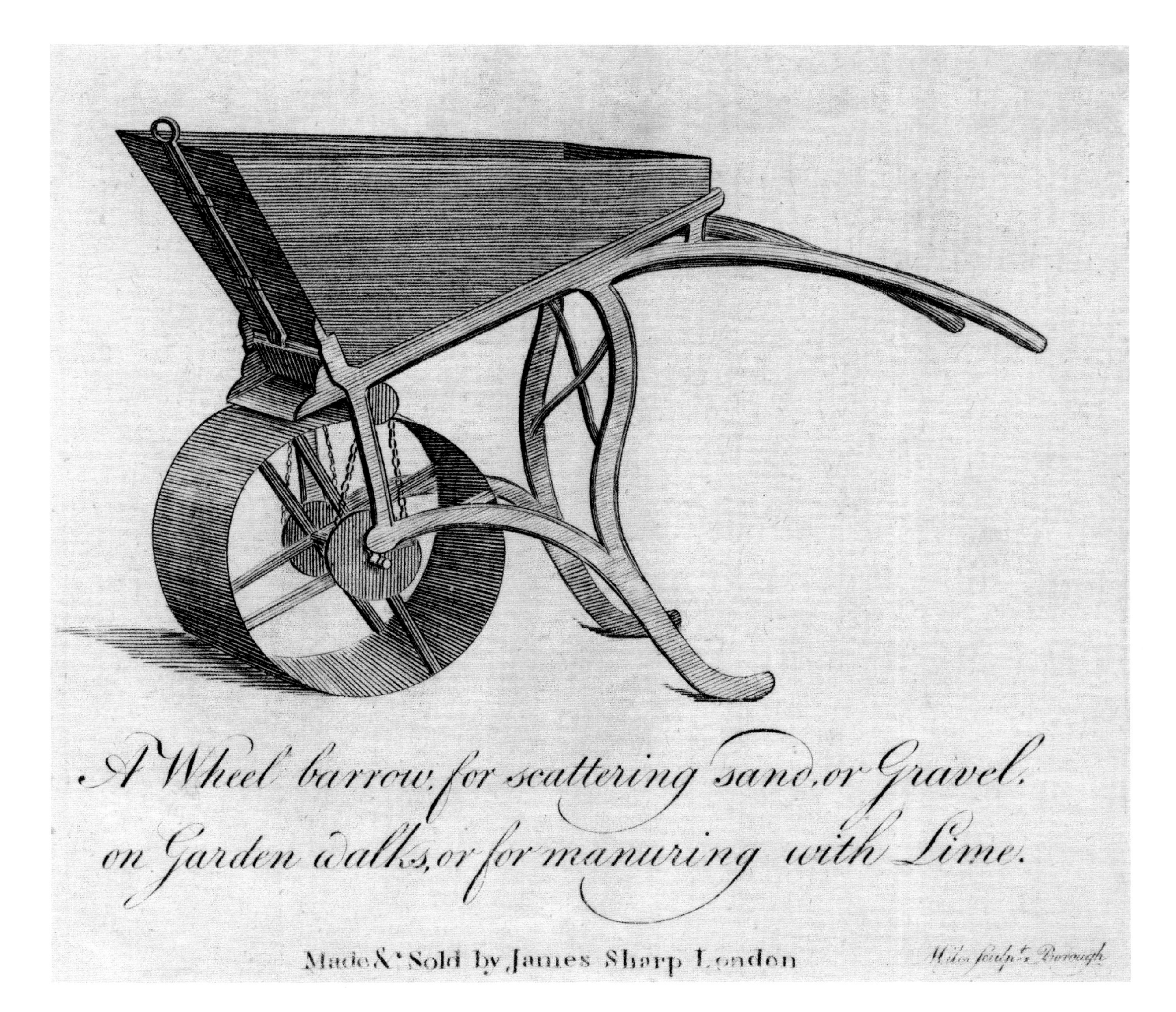
A Wheel barrow, for scattering sand, or Gravel.
on Garden walks, or for manuring with Lime.
Made & Sold by James Sharp London

LEFT
LANDSCAPE
Claude Lorrain

OPPOSITE
ABOVE THE LOWER LAKE,
June 2015

Many landowners of large estates were embracing a wider landscape. For some, it wasn't enough to just take land for a bigger garden, it was also worthy to emulate the works of William Kent, Charles Bridgeman and Capability Brown, and allow the garden to sprawl into the outer reaches of the estate. How much had been achieved at Belvoir is hard to tell. Judging by contemporary pictures, not much. But we do know that John of the Hill purchased drawing instruments in 1738 and a perspective glass in 1746. He also bought pictures by Gaspard Dughet (who later changed his name to Poussin) and Claude Lorrain[6] – artists whose work was known to have inspired landscape design at the time. (John of the Hill's grandson, the 4th Duke, was an avid collector in his own right and bought two more Claudes). Creating a sweeping landscape wasn't as easy to do as it looked. Brown was regularly tasked with rescuing earlier 'improvements' by ambitious landowners.

[6] Belvoir Archives – the 3rd Duke took an interest in Poussin and Claude, criticising various sale room attributions with annotations on the invoices: '*Flight into Egypt* called Claude Lorrain, rather Elsheimer in my opinion.' 17 guineas, 1745. And again: '*A Landscape Orion + Diana* by N. Poussin. G. [Dughet] Poussin in my opinion.' £31.10, 1745

Brown's surveyor, Jonathan Spyers, drew up extraordinarily accurate plans of the Estate as it was in 1779, ready for Brown to work on. Incredibly, our archivist, Peter Foden, only discovered Spyers' work while researching this book and, along with other plans, maps and drawings from both Spyers and Brown, we have been able to recognise the full scale and significance of their intentions. The sole surviving account book, part of a collection held at the RHS Lindley Library, Vincent Square, records:

A Survey of his Grace the Duke of Rutlands at Belvoir Castle taken by John Spyers in 1779 containing 3928 acres, and a very neat fair Drawing made of it with proper references to the Contents.

Mr Spyers Expences &c &c included at one shilling £196.08.00

Plans of the different Stories & Elevations of all the Fronts both to Belvoir Castle, & its Various offices taken by John Spyers, very accurately £20.00.00
A General Plan for the Alterations of the whole Place, among Plans & Elevations for the alterations of Belvoir Castle & its Various offices & for putting on an intire new attick story upon the Castle, all the Drawings made very descriptive, fair & neat, with Trees &c & bound into a book.

My journeys to Belvoir Castle & to Christmas 1782 included £300.00.00.

LEFT
FRONT COVER
of Brown's book of proposals for new designs for the Castle and landscape

ABOVE AND OPPOSITE
BROWN'S DESIGN
for the southwest elevation of the Castle

At first sight, Brown's plans appear to be typical of his grand ideas for transforming the landscape. The terraces climbing the steep mound that the Castle had perched on for the last 700 years were to be softened and a huge embankment connecting Castle Hill to another hill was to be built. His trademark ideas – lakes, drainage, areas flattened, others heightened, huge tracts of land to be wooded, clumps to be positioned and belts of trees to mark out the perimeter of the 2,300-acre Pleasure Grounds and parkland – were all planned. His architect's eye opened up areas to play with, regardless of whether the Duke owned the land or not. So far, so 'Brownian'. But as Brown expert, John Phibbs, tells us after studying the unusually large-scale plans in depth, they also seemed to be profoundly different.

Unlike much of his earlier work that saw villages wiped out for aesthetic purposes, Brown retained the village of Woolsthorpe, albeit behind a diaphanous tree belt, along with the ruined village church. Another departure from his *modus operandi*, which in the past had invited criticism, was to preserve the formal Tudor gardens, canal and Wilderness. Scope was created for a new Pleasure Ground with a walk and 'Shady Seat' (which later evolved into the Duchess's Garden and the Duke's Walk). But, most significantly, he had also become increasingly interested in matters mediaeval during the second half of his career. He intended to reinstate Belvoir's 'chase' (open land of great

OPPOSITE AND LEFT
ST. JAMES'S CHURCH, Woolsthorpe, at dawn

BELOW
ENGLISH OR GREY PARTRIDGE,
Watercolour by Nick Hugh McCann

distinction for hunting fallow and roe deer, foxes and pine martens with dogs) and the free warren (land granted by the Crown to hunt hare, rabbit, pheasant and partridge with a hawk) to echo the sentiments of Belvoir's genuine mediaeval history.

Belvoir had had a mediaeval free warren but the Estate never actually acquired a chase in the Middle Ages, which was much grander and also needed permission from the Crown. However, such a detail doesn't seem to have mattered to Brown.

There is sketchy evidence of a chase belonging to the Manor of Knipton, leased from the Duchy of Lancaster, in the 17th century. Many of the earlier Earls and Dukes of Rutland had 'assumed' the right to hunt deer in the 'chase' and the 4th Duke may well have influenced Brown's decision to elaborate the idea and create the vision of a chase. This would have given his Estate a superior setting. Chases required wide-open space with no fencing or walls. The park, farm and ridings had to be integrated much like other contemporary landscapes Brown was working on at the time, most notably Milton Abbey. Brown didn't plan any walls at Belvoir and we know that deer were free-roaming around the Castle as late as 1791;[7] all of it was open. By 1814, all the walls at Belvoir had been removed and entries in accounts were referring to 'Belvoir Chase', even though it was not a legal chase in the true sense.

We know that Brown was pleased with his finished scheme for Belvoir because he had talked to Horace Walpole, but Walpole's reaction was marred by his knowledge that the Duke was broke. In a letter to Lady Ossory, Walpole wrote: 'Mr Brown has shown his designs for improving Belvoir Castle. They show judgment and would be magnificent. I asked where the funds were to arise for I hear the Duke's exchequer is extremely empty.'[8]

7. J. Nichols, *The History and Antiquities of the County of Leicestershire*, 1795
8. Walpole correspondence

How far the 4th Duke intended to implement Brown's plan, we will never really know. We knew he had inherited enormous debts from his father and grandfather; he was already heavily in the red before he indulged his own penchant for collecting great works of art, gambling, women and entertaining.

What we didn't know was just how bad his situation was. A letter from Joseph Hill makes it clear: 'I conclude your Grace has received my List of your Debts – they are under-reckoned – & the Town Bills in particular instead of five thousand will be more than six [£780,000 today's equivalent] ... At present I see & know nothing, & am called upon to pay everything – a very unpleasant situation indeed! I forsee the inevitable Consequence – your Graces Noble Property will & must moulder away Piece Meal. Every part of your Estate is incumbered...'[9]

Another letter the following year continues on the same theme: 'I wish to see your Grace's present Debts payd & Your Income more than sufficient for your Annual Expences, & some Fund set apart & increasing for Payment of the great Debt on your Estates – A Vast Sum of Money is consumed in the Neighbourhood of Belvoir – that Estate has produced a mere trifle – Your Grace no Doubt enforces Economy there...'[10]

Joseph Hill was to be a sympathetic and persuasive influence on the 4th Duke. He had had many years of experience working for similar patrons whose estates were in peril. It wouldn't be an overstatement to suggest that his wisdom and advice, so deftly imparted, saved the Estate. But, even more pertinently, his work had brought him into close contact with several of Brown's patrons, including the Earl of Craven who had employed Brown at both Coombe Park in Warwickshire and Benham Park in Berkshire, and he had a first hand grasp of the landscaper's working methods for improving estates.

Brown's plans were finished in 1780 but because there wasn't any money little could be done immediately, although John Phibbs believes Brown did supervise some ground works. Tree planting started a couple of years later. A letter from the Duke's amanuensis, Thomas Thoroton, dated October 7th 1782, mentions Lucombe oaks being planted on the bottom of the northeast terrace above the ha-ha, opposite the stables, and notes: 'And is exactly conformable to Mr Brown's Plan, it is good ground for the Trees & they will be safe from the Deer.'[11] This may have been the work that Brown alluded to in his last letter to his client. But mounting debts, and the Duke's complete inability to face up to his responsibilities meant that, by 1784, Hill insisted that the only way to continue to run the Estate was if he implemented his own 'rescue plan'. The Duke agreed. He left for Dublin to take up the position of Lord Lieutenant of Ireland for a staggering salary of £20,000, although he was expected to forfeit about £15,000 in expenses. But how much he sent home was probably negligible. Hill, in the meantime, enforced a tight budget of £500 (£65,000 today) a year to be spent on the Estate and hypothecated money from the sale of timber from Belvoir's woodland to finance improvements.[12]

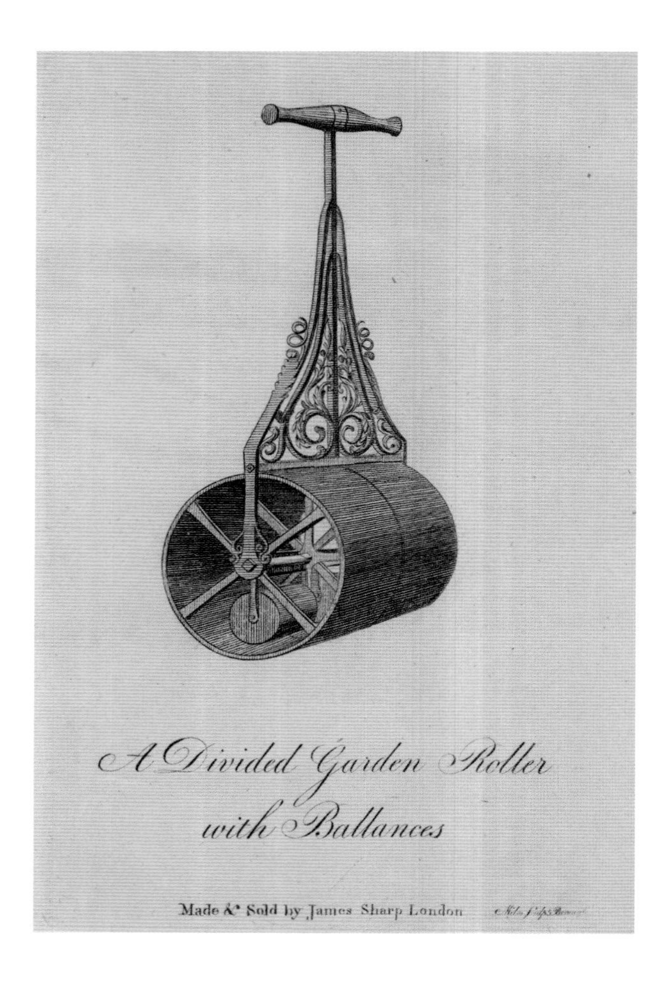

9. Belvoir Archives
10. Ibid.
11. Ibid.
12. Ibid.

The work eventually continued. Sacks of acorns were harvested in Croxton Park, between 1785 and 1787, and scattered on Woolsthorpe Hill as per the plan. Oaks do well in our heavy clay soil but young trees, transplanted from Croxton, under the supervision of head gardener, James Cook, worked better. Joseph Hill visited the Estate in April 1787: 'I had the Honour to come to your Grace's Castle last Friday, & have since been employed [with three of the Duke's agents:] Mr Thoroton, Mr Uppleby & Mr Fillingham in riding over various Parts of your Graces Property & considering Mr Brown's Plan & the Manner of executing it...The Plan I think will be a great Ornament to the Castle...It may however I apprehend be executed at a moderate Expence; & Trees are so many Years before they make any great Figure, that no Time should be lost in carrying the Plan into Execution.'[13] He went on to discuss how remaining enclosures could be made, which Brown had assumed would be acquired; who should help with drainage and how provision could be made for the building of the new roads so long as sand, stone and gravel could be quarried on the Estate.

OPPOSITE
GARDEN ROLLER with divided barrel and balances, 1773 (engraving)

LEFT
GARDENER HOEING
Pub. Erfurt in Thuringia, 1753-55 (engraving)
Christian Reicharts

Private Collection / The Stapleton Collection / Bridgeman Images

[13] Belvoir Archives

For the Duke, 1787 was surely an *annus horribilis*. Despite his virtual exile from Belvoir, he was still living extravagantly, drinking heavily and regularly frequenting Mrs Leeson's brothel in Pitt Street in Dublin – one infamous session lasted 16 hours, while his two aides-de-camp, armed with swords, waited outside for him on horseback. Then there were his affairs, the most notorious of which was with the opera singer, Elizabeth Billington. She was generous with her affections and shared them with the Duke's friend, the artist Joshua Reynolds, and the composer Joseph Haydn. The Duke had also, cheekily, found the wherewithal to liaise with Reynolds to purchase the *Seven Sacraments* by Nicolas Poussin for £2,000 (circa £4 million today). At the time, his priorities were sorely misjudged. Today, his art collection is a huge legacy. The paradox, of course, is that for all the trouble he got into buying them, the sale of two of his pictures in 2012 has supplemented our own finances to manage and maintain our heritage for the next generation. The same could also be said of his patronage to Brown, and the increased value of his investment today. But back then, Hill, with his wonderfully kind-hearted manner, still had his work cut out. The Duke was hopeless at responding to important correspondence and Hill knew that the Duke's deteriorating relationship with

ABOVE
'A SKETCH FROM NATURE', 1784, etching with stipple, Thomas Rowlandson

Royal Collection Trust /
© Her Majesty Queen Elizabeth II 2015

OPPOSITE
ORDINATION *c.* 1637-40 by Nicolas Poussin (detail). One of the series of seven pictures of the *Sacraments*

his wife, Mary Isabella had reached its nadir. Her solution was to leave him in Ireland and return to England. After everything she had endured, with a young family too, to have the Duke buying expensive paintings at the same time as telling her to save money on household expenses and her wardrobe must have been a low point. Hill wrote to him to sympathise with his 'Disorders of the Breast',[14] suggesting that his heavy use of claret was a bad medicine to deal with stress. For all the advice, not just from Hill but close members of his own family, the Duke succumbed to his demon, drink, and he died in October, 1787. But, despite everything, the Duke was a popular Lord Lieutenant of Ireland, if not hugely effectual, and he was remembered with fondness. The poet George Crabbe (also the Duke's private chaplain) praised him in his funeral address as a benevolent landowner.

[14] Belvoir Archives

Before the 4th Duke's death, Hill had also managed to engage Joseph Elkington, who was renowned for drainage and building roads, to start work at Belvoir. There is a suggestion in a letter from Hill to the 4th Duke that Henry Holland, Brown's son-in-law had been 'acquainted with [Brown's] Designs' for the rebuilding of the Castle too. But, at that stage, it was Frederick Trench, an old friend of the Duke's from Ireland (who had built Heywood House in County Laois and created a romantic demesne around it) who was to continue furthering the plans and develop a relationship with the family that continued well into the next generation.[15] Like the trustees of Brown's estate, Trench would also have to wait for his invoices to be paid...

John, the Duke's eldest son and heir was nine, and for the next 12 years, before he reached his majority at 21, his mother, Mary Isabella the Dowager and her brother, the Duke of Beaufort, were joint trustees for the Estate. It is more than possible that Beaufort and the Dowager were committed to executing the whole of Brown's plan. But legal constraints during the administration period prevented major investment. However, it was permissible to plant woodland, and fortunately Brown had planned a lot of woodland. Most of the perimeter belts of trees and several woods were planted during this period.

TWO SKETCHES OF THE CASTLE and grounds *c.* 1820, Col Frederick Trench. His father, also Frederick, had drawn up proposals for the new Castle. The Colonel was a great friend of the 5th Duke & Duchess and his artistic talents illustrate the development of the Pleasure Grounds

By the time the 5th Duke came of age in 1799 and brought his 18-year-old bride, Lady Elizabeth Howard to the Castle, fashions had changed. Picturesque was in vogue. It was a time to value beauty – as in Brown's smooth natural lines – together with the sublime – rocky, rugged, dramatic – in landscape architecture. Reaction to Brown's singular landscape was mounting. Even Jane Austen launched her displeasure in several of her novels, most notably in *Pride and Prejudice* where she gives Elizabeth Bennett the right to criticise Lord Darcy's garden at Pemberley, '...where natural beauty had been so little counteracted by an awkward taste'. Sir William Chambers, a rival of Brown's, wrote: 'A stranger is often at a loss to know whether he is walking in a meadow or in a pleasure ground, made and kept at very considerable expence.'[16] Uvedale Price was critical of his water features, saying: 'In Mr Brown's naked canals nothing detains the eye a moment, and the two sharp extremities appear to cut into each other. If a near approach to mathematical exactness was a merit instead of a defect, the sweeps of Mr Brown's water would be admirable.'[17]

Elizabeth was a prodigious reader and studied the work of many contemporary philosophers who wrote passionately about Picturesque landscape. She wrote in a letter to her husband on 23rd September, 1805, four years after work on the Castle and gardens had begun: 'I have read many books on planting [and] gardening, and in truth, I have therefore only had the common sense... to distinguish and find out many things that are going wrong here, I deserve no credit, I have only adopted the opinions of others which were perhaps the cleverest men of their age. For example, [of those] who wrote on gardening, [Edmund] Burke on the sublime, and beautiful, and [Uvedale] Price. It is [William] Mason's opinion that to be beautiful, [woods] ought to consist of the same sort of trees; entirely of oak or beech, I do not entirely agree with him'. She then went on to almost justify Brown's woodland planting schemes: 'The greatest fault of modern plant[ers] is their injudicious application of fir trees... [William] Shenstone who had more taste than any of them my friend Mason not excepted says, "they look like coronets on an elephant's back", when they are put on top of a hill, that idea made me laugh.' Incurably ambitious, Elizabeth's eye for fashion was unquestionable. She hated the neglected house and the staff who were nearly always drunk, and pursued her desire for a fairytale home with towers and turrets. During the 5th Duke's minority, the debts had been largely repaid and the family fortunes restored by their local coal mines and improved asset management. James Wyatt, fresh from his work at Windsor Castle, drew up new plans for the latest in Regency architectural mode and the Castle we see today is based, mostly, on both his work and that of Frederick Trench who had already started to adapt Brown's plan in 1784. Later additions were made by the Revd John Thoroton, the 5th Duke's private chaplain, personal friend and amateur architect.

Given that Elizabeth had such a strong feeling for design and architecture, it is not surprising that she had her own ideas for the gardens, too. There is evidence in the Belvoir Archives to suggest that Adam Mickle junior, who had formerly worked with Brown, may have also worked with James Wyatt while he was overseeing his work on the Castle. They had certainly ridden together over the Estate in 1799 with the 5th Duke.[18] Either way, it is clear that Elizabeth was building a sympathetic team of her own to enrich Brown's maturing planting schemes.

It seems the big picture for the landscape also had to take into consideration the feelings of the local populace. Elizabeth was more than aware of the unrest amongst the local working classes as they coped with hunger and poverty during the Napoleonic Wars, and adapted to the changes from the Industrial Revolution. The disastrous Castle fire in 1816 was always assumed, although never proven, to have been an arson attack by Luddites – protestors about labour-reducing technology in the textile trade. In a period fraught with the threat of revolution, Elizabeth embraced her important Tory political ideology of *noblesse oblige* and opened her home to the public.

15. Belvoir Archives
16. Sir William Chambers, *Dissertation on Oriental Gardening of 1772*
17. Uvedale Price, *An Essay on the Picturesque, as Compared with the Sublime and the Beautiful*; and on the *Use of Studying Pictures, for the Purpose of Improving Real Landscape*, revised edition. London, 1796
18. Belvoir Archives

Even 50 years after Elizabeth's death, many contemporary accounts marked the 'peculiar character of Belvoir, and one of its great charms, is that it stands in the midst of this open country, not within the confines of its own park. There is no enclosed park; and park palings, lodges, bolts, bars and locks are unknown. The Duke in his noble mansion, rests in the midst of his immense estates, and draws no cordon around him.'[19] As many as 5,000 visitors were flocking to the park from local, busy industrial towns during open days.

Elizabeth and the Duke were fair to their tenants and supportive of their needs and they took their privileges seriously. We found some lovely letters in the archives that sum up, too, how much Elizabeth enjoyed her role at Belvoir, and even more poignantly, how much fun she and her husband had working together. He is often considered to be rather long suffering, trailing in his wife's ambitious wake, but these letters to his agent, D'Ewes Coke, prove he was more than willing.

Date 3rd May, 1821: 'I am living alone here [Belvoir] with the Duchess & my Lady Bibi [sister] & we are having a very reasonable Life – At 12 o'clock, I ride with the Duchess to some of the neighbouring Village (Yesterday to Croxton, today to Redmile) where we plan & devise Improvements, call upon the Tenants to converse with them &c &c. The duchess has converted Croxton into a very pretty Village and the same will be to be said about Redmile, 'ere long...'[20] The Duke made his own contributions to the development of his new home, too, and was deliciously candid about some of the mediaeval fakery. He instigated the purchase of the armour that is displayed in the Guard Room and in another letter to D'Ewes Coke, he wrote: 'I am no historian myself, nor will any of my visitors be of that profession – My Ancestor in Henry 8th time may be supposed to have decorated his Hall with Armour & I in my time may store it with the arms peculiar to this age, viz Muskets, Swords, &c – as we mold the Castle to give it the appearance of Antiquity & we take our ideas from our Ancestors in that Respect, where is the harm of Old Armour in a Hall intended to look as if it belonged to days of yore?'[21]

By the time Elizabeth died, in 1825, she had rebuilt the Castle, endured the implications of the devastating fire in 1816 and subsequent rebuilding, overseen Brown's embankment going up, the lakes prepared and dammed (although, sadly never saw them filled), thrown her energies into her Model Farm in the parkland, added village greens on the Estate, furnished cottages with gardens, built grottos and opened the gardens to the public. And given birth to 10 children.

To conclude, the gardens and parkland today are very much Brown's, started under the auspices of the 4th Duke, continued by his widow Mary Isabella and her brother the Duke of Beaufort, finished by Elizabeth, and crafted by a host of wonderfully pioneering and inspired head gardeners, the occasional headstrong Duchess and fashion. But, most importantly, because of this gradual and thorough process, they fit the modern needs of a 21st century agricultural estate. I also have a strong feeling that the sudden and untimely death of Elizabeth had perhaps inspired her husband and her children, who included both the 6th and 7th Dukes, to preserve her greatest monument: Belvoir Castle and gardens. However, by the time the 8th Duke came to Belvoir in 1906, the old associations with Elizabeth had been buried with his father, the last member of that generation. It's perhaps not surprising that Violet, the 8th Duke's artistic wife, was ready to embrace innovative technology and update the Castle, and apply her own very considerable creative talents to parts of the gardens. After Violet, Frances, the present Dowager Duchess of Rutland, has made significant improvements and I have been lucky to carry on with my own.

OPPOSITE
VIOLET, DUCHESS OF RUTLAND, 1896 (detail), Sir James Jebusa Shannon. A hugely talented artist, she was a member of the aristocratic intellectuals known as 'The Souls'. This stunning painting of her shows her in the act of drawing, as 'Egeria', her nickname, the wise nymph of mythology

Bridgeman Images / Private Collection

[19] Llewellyn Jewitt and Samuel Carter Hall, *The Stately Homes of England*, 1874
[20] Belvoir Archives
[21] Ibid.

CHAPTER TWO

THE FORMAL TERRACES

When we have people staying at the Castle, the buzz around the breakfast table is nearly always about the spectacular views out of the bedroom windows, especially if it's a first visit or they arrived in the dark. But many guests have been surprised by the lack of an obvious garden. Depending which window you're looking out of, you could easily skim over the only formal gardens which are sited on skinny terraces below the Castle battlements. We do not covet conventional lawns, beds and borders and all the accoutrements of a stately pile; we simply don't have the right topography – or huge numbers of gardeners. Brown's gardens were 'gardenless', dramatic landscapes, and ours is no exception. For every traditional garden feature, Belvoir multiplies it over and over again. Take, for example, an ordinary herbaceous border with its ever-changing shapes, colours and scents and scale it up – Belvoir style – and you have vast theatrical woodland gardens that deafen with birdsong, are alive with wildlife and shimmer with iridescence from late January with snowdrops and early camellias through to May with waves of striking pinks, dazzling reds and the many other colours of our growing collection of rhododendrons. An ornamental fishpond becomes one of many water features, from the grand lakes to the newly dredged trout ponds. Sweeping lawns and clipped edges are replaced with huge stretches of grassy parkland (for grazing animals) with the occasional ha-ha and hedge, all loosely hemmed in by Capability Brown's roughly 10-mile tree belt. But we do have formal gardens that can be strolled around. All the actual planting has been designed by others within Brown's framework for Pleasure Grounds. And we have some remarkable people to thank for their horticultural and botanical contributions.

THE TUDOR TERRACE

My tour starts from the front door. The actual mound of earth that the Castle is perched on is only big enough to accommodate the foundations and a slim car park before it falls steeply away, behind the battlements and down the hill. There must always have been a spiral driveway to the Castle but it's likely that the terraces were cut into the slope over 450 years ago. Brown proposed to soften all the terraces, which didn't happen, but in his plan he kept the same Spiral Walk that winds around Castle Hill. It takes about 10 or 15 minutes to wander through – if you don't stop much to admire the views and feel the breeze in your hair. As the levels descend into the woodlands, the air becomes stiller, the birdsong increases and the scents from the tapestry of colours from all the woodland planting can be intoxicating.

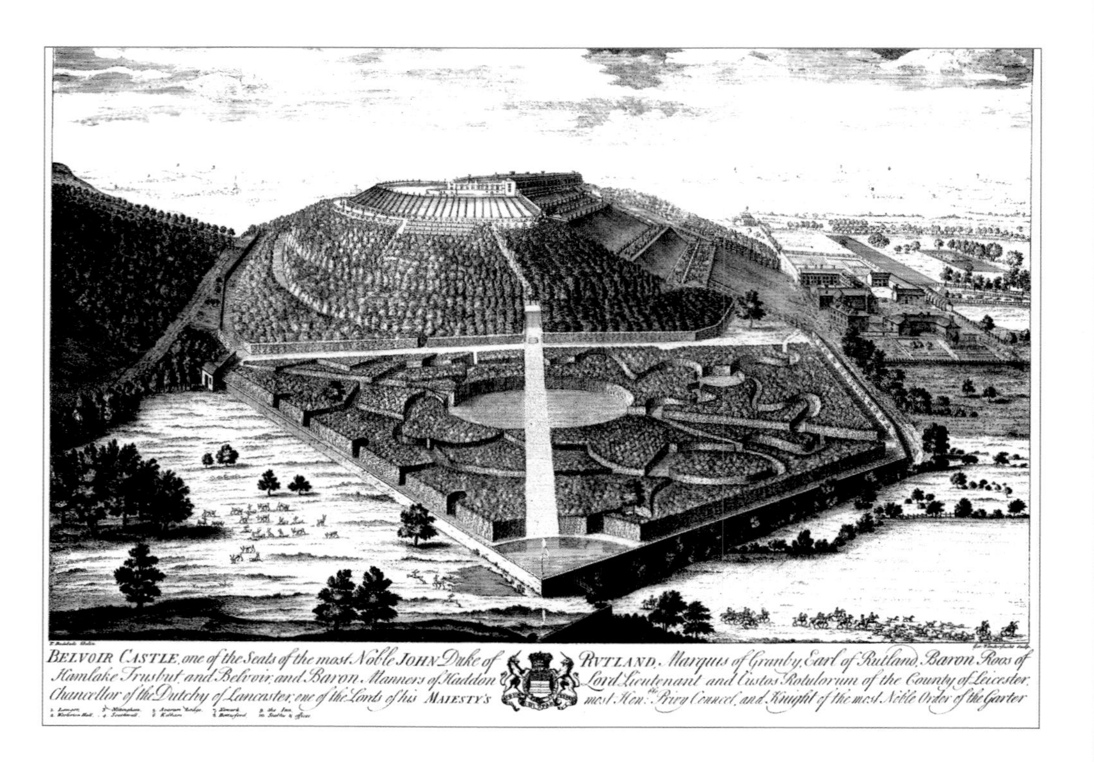

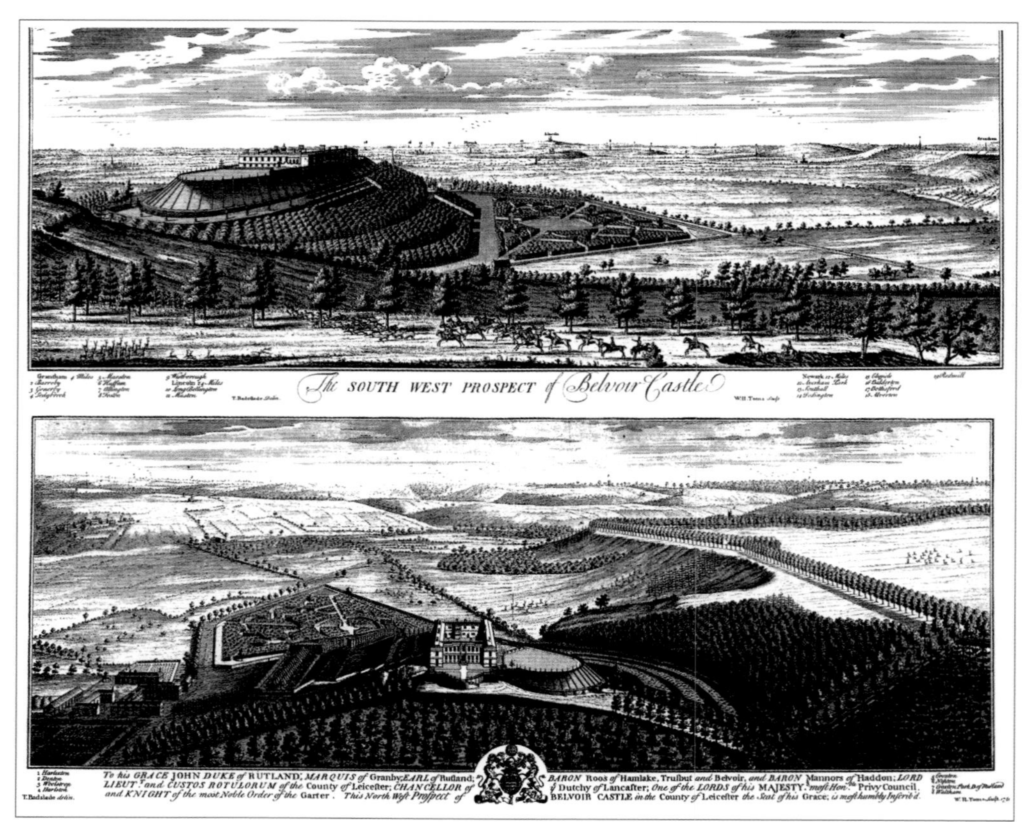

PREVIOUS PAGES
SOUTH FRONT OF THE CASTLE
and a view looking south towards Knipton

RIGHT
THREE PROSPECTS OF
BELVOIR CASTLE 1731
at the time of John Manners,
3rd Duke of Rutland. Top: the elaborate knot gardens on the northeast terraces and the huge formal wilderness

From *Vitruvius Britannicus*, J. Badeslade, J. Rocque, John Woolfe & James Gandon

OPPOSITE
AERIAL VIEW, March 2015

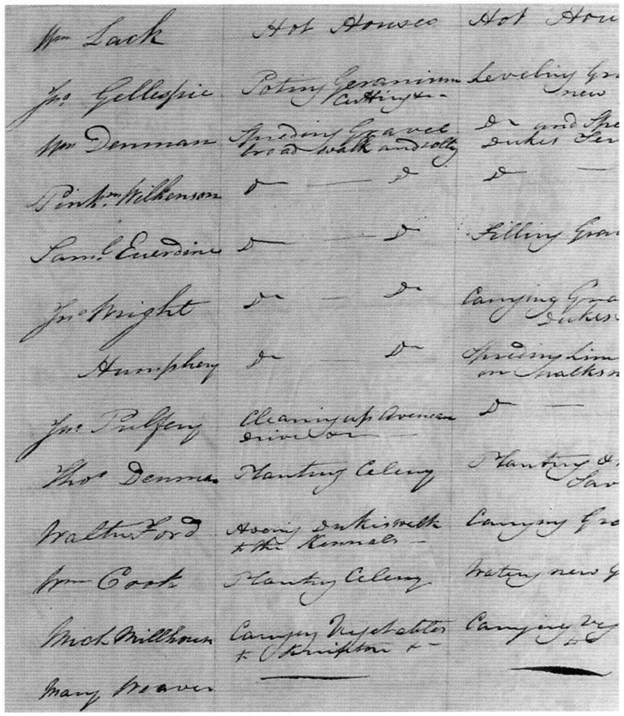

Wm Lack	Hot Houses	Hot Hou[illegible]
Jno Gillespie	Poting Geranium Cuttings	Leveling [illegible] new
Wm Denman	Spreading Gravel broad walk and [illegible]	do and Spre[illegible] Dukes [illegible]
Pink Wilkenson	do — do	do —
Saml Everdine	do — do	Filling Gra[illegible]
Jno Wright	do do	Carrying Gra[illegible] Dukes
Humphrey	do do	Spreading Lim[illegible] on Walks
Jno Pulfery	Cleaning up Avenue drive	do —
Thos Denman	Planting Celery	Planting [illegible]
Walther Ford	Hoeing Dukes walk & the Kennels	Carrying [illegible]
Wm Cook	Planting Celery	Watering new [illegible]
Mich Millhouse	Carrying [illegible]	Carrying [illegible]
Mary Weaver		

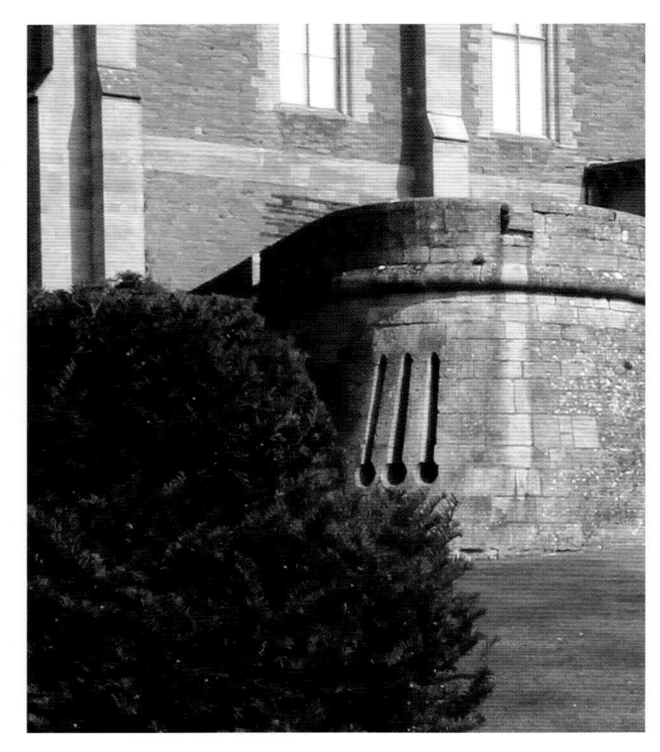

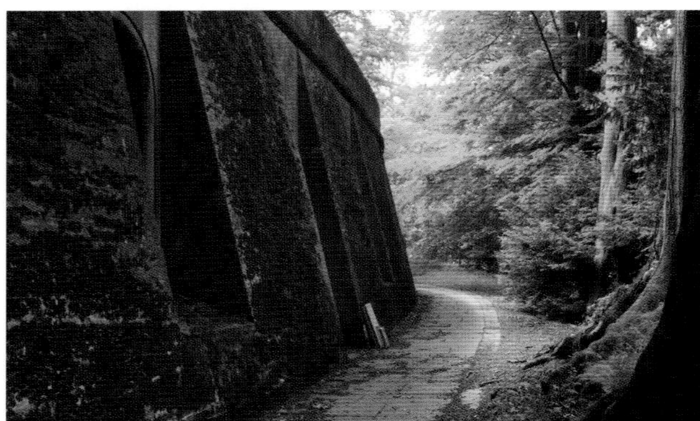

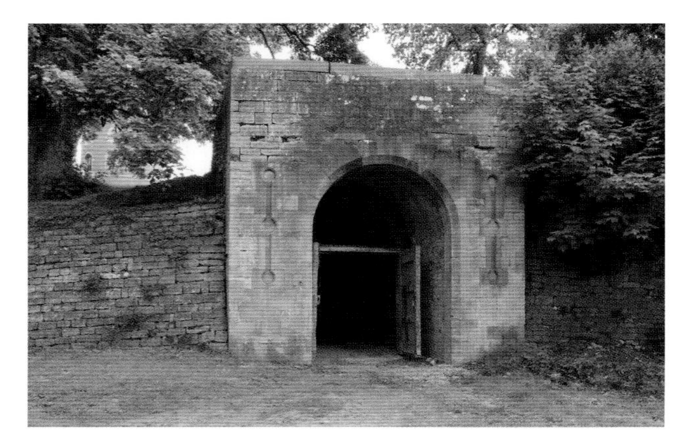

ABOVE
PAGE DETAIL from the Belvoir Under Gardeners and Labourers book for July 1818

RIGHT (top to bottom)
THE DOOMS ARE ILLUMINATED by slits to be seen in the southwest stone promontary;
THE PATHWAY FROM THE DOOMS to the subterranean workshops;
THE DOOMS ENTRANCE

OPPOSITE
A FEAT OF EARLY 19TH CENTURY ENGINEERING, the Dooms extend to around 100 metres

From the front door on the northeast terrace, past the Rose Garden, which we will come back to, we come to the Dooms. The rather ominous name was given to the 'subterranean passage' on Brown's plans – the tradesmen's entrance into the Castle. As well as produce, coal was transported straight from the family's Derbyshire mines via the Grantham canal, loaded onto wagons and brought directly into the Castle under this passageway.

We don't know why they became known as the Dooms but a clue could be in the name. According to the Ledgers in the Belvoir Archives, John Dodson & Company was employing eight men on the Estate at the time, and the company invoiced for 'a Subterranean Passage to the Coal Yard at 7d per yard,' between March and October 1803 using a gang wagon and railways. It's interesting that they weren't using horses but the work would still have been gruelling, even with modern engineering to transport the spoil away. Health and safety laws were obviously centuries away and accidents must have been common. No records were kept except for deaths and one entry in the spring of 1803 records the tragic death of the unfortunate Mr Worsdale of Woolsthorpe while working in the tunnel. He left a wife and two children. An entry by his name in the Ledgers suggested assistance should be given to the family via an annual Benefaction.

You come out at the old ice-house, and the subterraneous workshops which are now the gardener's sheds and loos, and follow the Spiral Walk round to the top of three impressively deep terraces. After the dissolution of the monasteries, power shifted from Belvoir Priory, established in 1077, and its wealth was transferred to the family in the 1540s. It's likely that the 2nd Earl of Rutland had these terraces dug out and furnished them with elaborate knot gardens similar to the sketches in *Vitruvius Britannicus* (see page 62). Our next garden project may well be to tackle the Tudor gardens, and these terraces will be the first on the job list.

For now, we have started with the new pleached-hornbeam pathway that was planted in autumn 2015. The view over the swimming pool and tennis court looks straight ahead to the stables that were completed in 1704 and built to complement the third Castle. They replaced earlier ones that had been used as barracks by Cromwell's soldiers during the Civil War. Inside the rotunda is an indoor horse walker that was added in the late 19th century. There are only three others like it in the country.

The 8th Duke's wife, Violet, had a passion for modernising the Castle – embracing electricity and plumbing when she moved into Belvoir with her husband in 1906 on the death of her late father-in-law, the 7th Duke. And she loved gardening, too. Violet was a great beauty, and one of the original Souls: an informal group of aristocratic politicians, intellectuals and artists. Her own artistic talents were impressive. Many of her drawings and portraits are on the walls in the Castle. But her finest work was the sculpture of her dead son, Lord Haddon. It was exhibited at the Tate Gallery before it came to the Chapel at Belvoir. We are fortunate that she kept records of all the changes she made, both inside and out, in her notebook titled *Additions to Belvoir by VR 1906-1925.*

OPPOSITE
AN AERIAL VIEW clearly shows the entrance to the Dooms, lower right

FAR LEFT
VIOLET, the 8th Duke's wife with her children

LEFT
VIOLET'S SCULPTURE of the recumbent figure of her son, Lord Haddon

She regularly added titbits of information about plants or stone furniture she had moved, with one such entry recording: 'Looking down on Rotunda on the level of those wonderful Ilexes is a big stone square trough (from down behind the Stable Pond) Heavy to lift.' Her notes have a real working journal feel to them, and I often read them and then go off excitedly in search of things she's mentioned, only to find that they have gone. But then three other Duchesses have also been here before me.

The tennis court is a good example. Violet wrote: 'The lawn tennis ground – I built a summer house – thatched – & of a shape I copied from a summer house on the Duke's Walk.' The tennis court has been tarmacked at least twice since the days of rolling a grass one.

The Woolsthorpe avenue lies in the distance above the stables and, on a clear day, you can see as far as Lincoln Cathedral. Just to the right of the stables is the eight-acre kitchen garden designed by Elizabeth in 1816. She also planted the cedars, and poplar trees (now gone), and a shrubbery to hide the workman-like red brick walls of the new kitchen gardens.

Since 2001, when we moved in, sheep have continued to graze the hill in the Brown tradition but, in 2013, when we started our restoration programme, we planted evergreen magnolias (*Magnolia grandiflora*) on the huge and rather ugly wall that holds up the Castle

on this northeast terrace. Inevitably, the sheep got through the fencing and ate them, and so we had to start again in 2014.

The grass here could have been scythed or sheared to a bowling green finish when Brown planned these Pleasure Grounds, but it would have been an expensive and labour-intensive exercise. Instead, by fencing groups of trees and shrubs, the areas would have been grazed. This was common practice and was widely recognised as an acceptable method of trimming during the first half of the 18th century. Except for occasionally, as when Anne Temple reported her aunt's fear that the sheep would escape in a letter to Richard Grenville in 1750: 'I went to my Lady Cobham yesterday and she begin in a violent manner about the Sheep being put into the garden [at Stowe]... she told Brown she had cry'd all night and never slept a wink about it...'[22]

A similar calamity was reported at Belvoir. Elizabeth wrote to her husband from Brighton, on 31st September, 1804: 'I have at last heard from Mr Thoroton..., he seems to think things are not going on very well at Belvoir, I do not mean the building, for I am perfectly convinced everything Mr Turner has to do with must go on well, but he tells me, that as usual they let the cattle in among the trees, I am quite vexed for I thought I had said enough on that subject to Mr King [agent] before I left Belvoir.'[23]

There is some small comfort to take from these two stories when I think of the unnecessary expense of replanting our magnolias.

OPPOSITE (from top)
THE ROTUNDA (horse walker) was added in the late 19th century to the existing 17th century stable block;
SHEEP GRAZE the northeast terrace above and below the tennis court;
LINCOLN CATHEDRAL seen in the distance from the Castle terrace

ABOVE
WOOLSTHORPE AVENUE of limes and St. James's Church

22. Letter from Anne Temple to Richard Grenville (afterwards Earl Temple), 1750
23. Belvoir Archives

As the Spiral Walk leads you away from the northeast terrace to the private terraces you reach a junction in garden paths, where from 1730 the family would have strolled down the hill to their new garden: the Wilderness. At the time, John of the Hill and his family would have enjoyed the very latest in garden fashion. However, despite its wealth and position, the family had already endured more than its fair share of grief – by 1730, John's poor wife Bridget, aged 30, had already lost six of her children: four daughters and two little boys. By the time she died four years later, her husband and only five of her 11 children survived her. It is a sad and recurring theme in all the gardens here – over the generations many, many children have died and the Duchesses of their day must have spent much time in quiet reflection gathering solace from the peace and timeless beauty of their surroundings.

The heyday of wilderness gardens was in the 1680s, but the style had a renaissance after the Gothic garden designer, Batty Langley, filled a book in 1728 of designs boasting exotic plants and walkways. It's possible that our site was chosen to update an existing maze that is recorded in 1540 without a precise location, or there may even have been some woodland there that needed titivating. But it is more likely that John of the Hill, who had acquired lands at Knipton through an Enclosures agreement in 1727, was able to divert a road away from the bottom of the Castle and make way for an ornamental feature. The timing couldn't have been better to show off the latest horticultural must-have. Our wilderness has two principal walks on the diagonal with a serpentine 'arti-natural' circuit. It would have been the perfect spot to amble round before walking back home up the hill. If you can fight your way into the overgrowth, the structure still exists. Brown, who in his earlier works was always quick to strike out existing formal gardens, left the Wilderness as well as the Tudor canal and adjacent gardens. Maybe he could see its potential for neglect and would know that it wouldn't take long before it blended into his plan, just as it, and the Tudor Gardens, do now.

At some time before 1825, all these walks were separated from the surrounding parkland, and the Wilderness, by Brown's ha-ha wall – albeit in a tighter embrace to the Castle than on his plan. There are several clumps of yew trees at the bottom of these southeasterly terraces, which are attributed to him, and several sweet chestnuts straddling the ha-ha. They would have been planted before the ha-ha went in, possibly as a nuttery, set out in a grid. Brown's plan led to reshaping the clump to frame views out to the site of a

'mysterious grotto' (now gone) in the woods behind Wyatt's Dairy, which we think may have been part of the Arcade Walk that is mentioned in the Ledgers but without any explanation as to where it was.

We often have to accept that we might never find the answers to some mysteries in our gardens. Similarly, it seems, we have to expect surprises of all kinds in the gardens, too, like the time a guide once reported the story of a volunteer gardener weeding above the ha-ha close to the Wilderness. Nothing extraordinary in that, but unbeknown to anyone he was a naturist and the guide had to smartly tell him to put his clothes on before the public arrived.

We are indebted, and incredibly grateful, to our volunteers for the work they have done. Many are highly skilled gardeners who, working closely with our own gardeners Nikki Applewhite and Martin Gibbs, have clocked up over 4,500 hours of labour during the restoration programme.

OPPOSITE
ABOVE THE HA-HA in spring the woodland is a riot of bluebells and rhododendrons

LEFT
A CARPET OF SNOWDROPS on the slope of the north facing terrace

CHAPTER THREE

THE 'ANCIENT' TERRACES

Following the Spiral Walk from the north terrace takes you to the bottom of three southwest facing private terraces. Flanked from above by two turrets, these terraces are the oldest part of all the gardens. The earliest evidence reports vineyards growing at Belvoir in 1200 and again in the 1700s. Timothy Thomas, chaplain to Lord Oxford, described them in 1725: 'Upon ye sides of it is an indifferent Sort of Gardening, divided into Sevll Slopes: Here are Vines upon reclining brick walls, which have stoves underneath to force their ripeness.'[24]

Even without stoves, on a frosty day in the middle of winter, if the sun is out, these terraces are warm. If only these ancient sloping walls that have been holding the Castle in place for hundreds of years could talk. It is certainly easy to imagine wistful thoughts of earlier ladies, countesses and duchesses taking their constitution up and down the garden levels. Violet wrote about the private Terrace Gardens in her notebook (between 1907 and 1914): 'The three Stone Terraces below the Southern side were much loved by Henry 8th Duke and His Father – in my day – They kept adding treasures. The Magnolias were I thought the best of anything. There is one plant I call 'Crotegus' – for I knew it as a Child in the Pyrenees – I found in an old letter – from the 1st Lady John Manners' mother Mrs Marlay – to the 6th Duke a mention of sending him a plant of this white flowered – red leaved shrub – for his Terrace. And I think I discovered it still flourishing.'

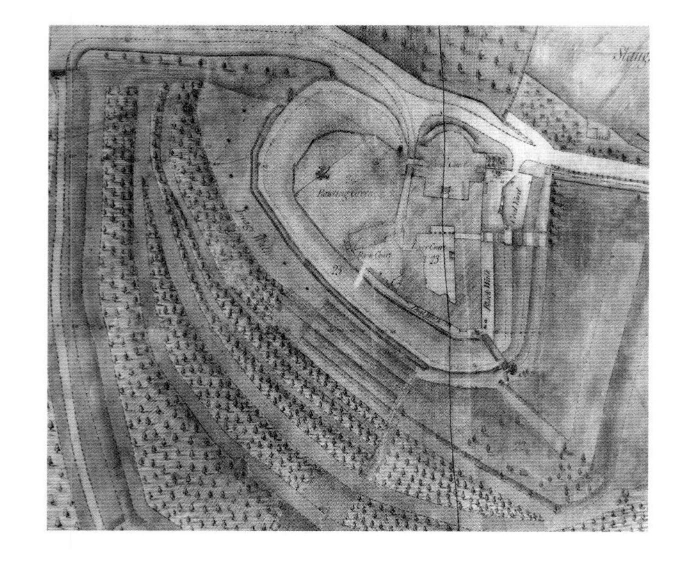

RIGHT
A DETAIL OF THE 1799 MAP showing the ancient terraces – just before John Henry and Elizabeth began their remodelling. Showing that Brown's plan for the Castle and its hill had not been implemented

OPPOSITE
THE TOP TERRACE with one of the two Gothic towers which flank the terraces

[24] Timothy Thomas Journal, 1725

THE KITCHEN GARDEN

The sloping wall at the bottom of the terraces lends itself to a small and homespun kitchen garden. It's a far cry from the eight-acre walled kitchen garden that Elizabeth built, now used as a horse paddock, but we are at least able to grow some of our own fruit and vegetables, which is very rewarding. Although we haven't tried to grow edible grapes, we have a beautiful, ornamental purple-leaved vine that grows on the wall today, and our white peaches, Avalon Pride (*Prunus persica*) have been very successful.

ABOVE
MAGNOLIAS ARE A FEATURE of the terraces in spring

OPPOSITE & RIGHT
A MODEST KITCHEN GARDEN
is perfectly situated in this warm south-facing spot

THE BOTTOM TERRACE

This terrace is even skinnier than the other terraces on this side of the Castle. Because of the micro-climate in these gardens, we thought we'd have a bit of fun with some tropical plants. The foxglove tree (*Paulownia tomentosa*), with its huge leaves spanning about 40cms, and the rice-paper plant (*Tetrapanex papyrifer*), from Taiwan, again with huge leaves up to 50cms across, are real treats. The latter is particularly special as it's very difficult to grow this far north because it gets too cold, but ours is thriving in this warm, sheltered spot. We have transplanted some suckers into the new rockery in the Duchess's Garden and they have adapted well.

TOP & OPPOSITE
THE SLIMMEST LOWER TERRACE
is no less spectacular for that

ABOVE
DECORATIVE URNS
provide elegant symmetry on the private walkway below the terraces

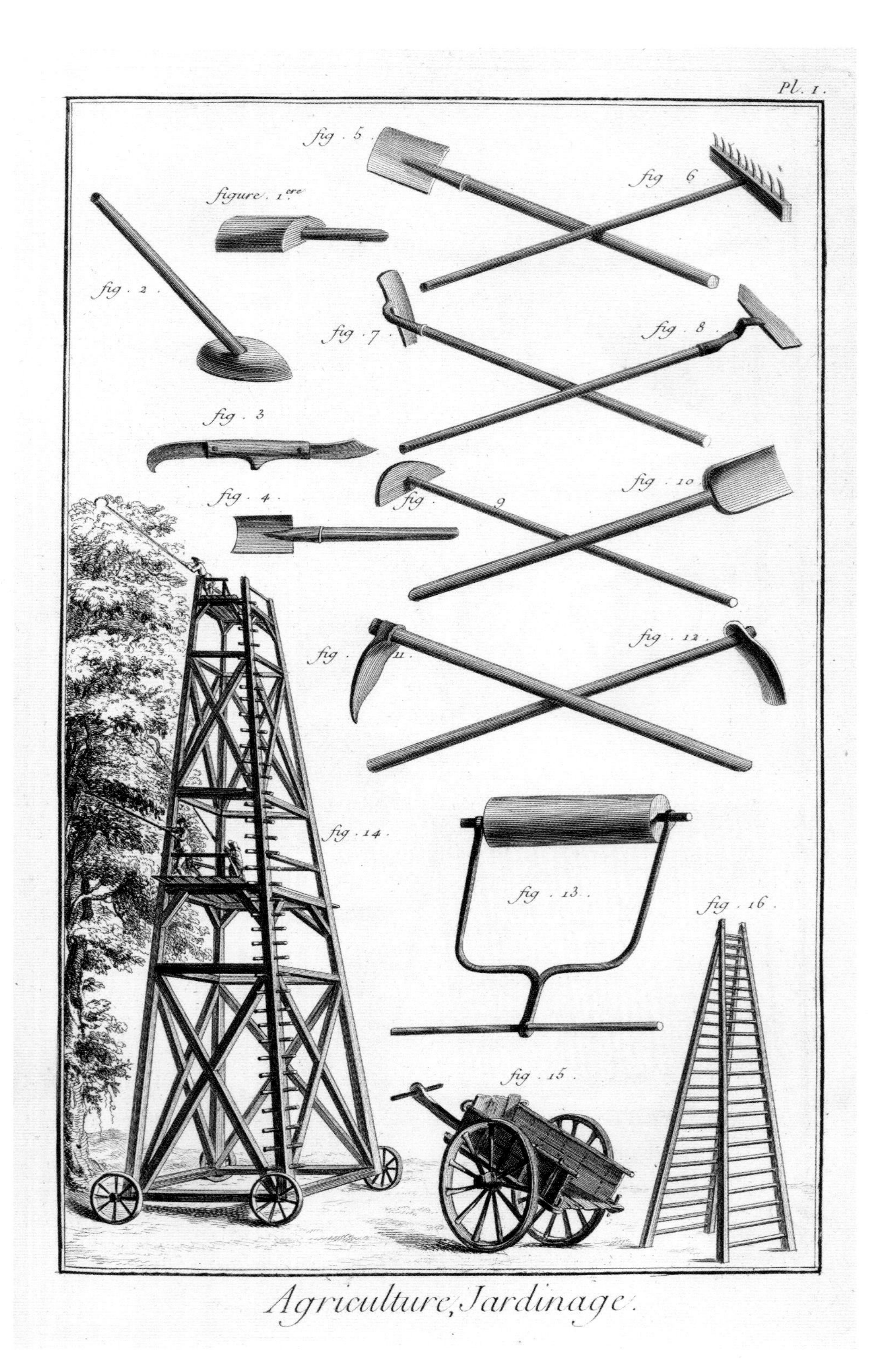

LEFT
'AGRICULTURE JARDINAGE'
18th CENTURY GARDENING TOOLS and a mobile pruning platform from the *Encyclopedie des Sciences et Metiers*, Denis Diderot (1713-84) published c.1770

Private Collection / The Stapleton Collection / Bridgeman Images

TOP
A PRUNING LADDER lies next to the vast Ceanothus

OPPOSITE
MAGNIFICENT MAGNOLIAS still flourish from Duchess Violet's time

THE MIDDLE TERRACE

Of all these terraces, this is my favourite. It is more-or-less totally private; many people don't even know where it is, which suits us perfectly. The magnolias that Violet refers to are still here and they are as magnificent in spring as ever.

In the Victorian era, this was the Flower Garden Terrace, an area for the gardeners to showcase their skills, and they packed as many blooming shrubs and spring flowers in as they could. The brief would have been simple: to provide spring colour in the gardens while the family was in residence for the hunting season. Each gardener would have had his own style,

but the most notable are William Ingram, head gardener between 1878 – 1894, and Mr W H Divers from 1894 to 1917. Divers was well known amongst horticultural circles, winning the Royal Horticultural Society gold medals for fruit. It's difficult to think of him getting muddy when you read an account of his character by Lady Diana Cooper, daughter of the 8th Duke and Duchess. She wrote: 'Mr. Divers, the head gardener, had a black W. G. Grace beard covering his chest, a black cut-away coat, Homburg hat and a bunch of Bluebeard keys. It was impossible to imagine a spade in his hands.'[25] But a spade, and much more besides, he must have held. With the help of 40 under gardeners, he oversaw two and three-quarter-acres of vegetable culture in the walled kitchen gardens, providing for 130 people in residence, grown alongside both spring bedding and herbaceous borders for cut flowers for the house. But it was his spring planting and continuation of his predecessor, Mr Ingram's use of massed areas of spring bulbs, that are his greatest legacy.

Spring flowers were essential at Belvoir to provide colour during the hunting season. Until the 9th Duke's day, the family was only in full-time residence during the winter for hunting and shooting and, as soon as the season closed, they left for other estates and their London houses, thereby not needing horticultural decoration during the summer months. The 8th Duke was so inspired by his gardeners' success that he commissioned a book by Divers to record the most successful plants and bedding – *Spring Flowers at Belvoir Castle, with Directions for Cultivation and Notes, on the Gardens.* It was to be the best record of its kind and inspired many of the parks in the industrial north at the time.

In his book, Divers describes this terrace as the Flower Garden Terrace with a traditionally planted flower garden where magnolias covered the Castle walls. The glorious magnolias still grace the walls from early April and the rambling *Rosa banksiae* 'Lutea' with abundant sprays of small, pale yellow double blooms, originally bred by Lady Banks (1825), still survives.

When we came to freshen up the terrace in 2005, many of the plants were old and weak, and the weeds were rampant. I remembered seeing an old picture, somewhere, of this terrace with scallop shaped flowerbeds. The width of the terrace is only a matter of feet and the design works well. If I had my time again, I would have made the turret below the terrace into the front door to our private apartment and made this the front garden.

OPPOSITE
EMMA, DUCHESS OF RUTLAND reads Divers' book, strolling on the Middle Terrace – Lady Banks' rose, behind (not in flower)

LEFT
LADY DIANA COOPER and her beloved Beddingtons on the Top Terrace, 1923

25. Lady Diana Cooper, *The Rainbow Comes and Goes*, Rupert Hart-Davis, 1958. Lady Diana Manners married Duff Cooper, 1st Viscount Norwich, politician, cabinet minister, diplomat, writer and diarist

THE TOP TERRACE

This is the spot where, for almost as far the eye can see, the view is exactly that which Brown planned. On warm days we throw open the terrace doors onto the grassed terrace where we have recently replaced tired lavender shrubs with pale pink roses called 'The Fairy' and low growing catmint (*Nepeta racemosa)* 'Walkers Low' between box buttresses. When we first moved in, in 2001, the whole terrace was gravelled right up to the battlements and covered in dog mess, so I asked a friend and wonderful garden designer, Caroline Lomas to plant something that would remind our very young children of their old back garden at Knipton Lodge, a mile away. They missed the freedom of walking into the garden and just rolling on grass or jumping on a swing, and playing with the dogs. She ripped up the tired old gravel, rolled out squares of turf and planted lavender as deeply as looked sensible, to deter the children from climbing over the top and falling five metres to the three terraces below.

Our dogs' kennels were placed in one corner, which made the garden feel like home, and it was a perfect place for the climbing frame and swings. As the children have grown up, the dogs have commandeered the space as an extension to their kennels and we're still picking up dog mess; some things never change.

It's really the Arcadian views from here that steal the show. For me they completely sum up Brown's brilliance. It was for a very good reason that Brown switched the focus of the views from the north and east to this far more pleasing, not to say warmer, aspect. And, as a result, the family's living areas were rearranged too. As Joseph Hill commented to the 4th Duke in a letter in 1787, Brown's plan would be a great ornament to the Castle, 'though unfortunately the greater Part of the Water & Plantations will not front the present Sitting Rooms.'[26] James Wyatt's plans did not contradict Hill's thoughts and we have him and the 5th Duke and Duchess to thank for considering Brown's views when they chose where to position their principal private sitting rooms. From many of our private rooms, almost as far as the eye can see, the view is Brownian. (The only exception, however, is the Hunt Kennels, built for the 5th Duke to a design by James Wyatt in 1802). The Lakes are straight ahead and, although somewhat different in place and size, are swollen from the River Devon as he intended. The Brewer's Grave approach (allegedly named after a Castle servant who drowned in a vat of ale that he was brewing) crosses the river over a very Brownian styled bridge, which was completed just before Elizabeth died in 1825. The drive then traverses up the hill towards the gates on the Denton road.

The village of Woolsthorpe to the north, below the tree plantations in Cliff Wood, is still visible. Although Brown had planned a thin tree belt to screen it from certain angles, it's difficult to tell if the trees were ever planted as there aren't any old ones left there now. The Duke of Beaufort seemed so enamoured with the look of the village that he even had a white steeple mounted on the village church in about 1795, which stayed up until it was rebuilt in 1845 with a tower. Following the tree line to the south is the cemetery of St. James's Church, the ruins of which Brown had saved as a monument to his Gothic taste, but which were finally razed to the ground by Elizabeth. Where the tree belt stopped we filled in the gap and planted over 5,800 trees in 2015 as a gesture to mark Brown's tercentenary. Beneath the new plantation are the Memorial Lakes that we

rebuilt during 2014-2015 from original ponds that were dug out in 1826.

Continuing the view into the distance towards the village of Croxton Kerrial, in a clockwise direction, are the late 18th-century tree plantations called Croxton Bank – a popular fox cover and pheasant shelter, and Cedar Hill, perched high up on a hill and aptly named after Brown's clump of cedar of Lebanon trees planted in accordance with Beaufort's wishes: '15 feet Distance – Scotch firs may be mixed with them, which may be taken up afterwards when the Cedars are Grown – The Ground to be first plow'd'. Thomas Whately, a writer and associate of Brown's, describes these outer landscape touches as: 'Clumps of woods in the view, denote the neighbourhood of a seat'.[27]

In places, you can just make out the position of Croxton Avenue, Brown's private carriage drive from the Castle to Croxton Park, which was begun in 1802, and has the classic characterisation of a riding. Queen Victoria, Prince Albert and Queen Adelaide (widow of William IV) and the 5th Duke travelled along it in a carriage drawn by four horses and attended by outriders dressed in his Grace's livery for a Belvoir Hunt meet at Croxton Park in 1843.

Brown's perimeter belt is picked up again from Knipton at King's Wood and Granby Wood, as the eye travels round to the west and Briery Wood in the foreground, bringing you back to where we started with immediate views below the parapet and the Flower Garden Terraces.

26. Belvoir Archives
27. Thomas Whateley, *op. cit.*

CHAPTER FOUR

THE 'MODERN' TERRACES

By contrast to the 'ancient' terraces on the southeast side of the Castle, this next set of terraces, lying to the right of the main drive and the Castle's front door, seems comparatively modern. They have probably changed more times than any other part of the entire landscape and Brown was quick to make his own changes here, too.

It was here that he indulged his enthusiasm for earthmoving better than anywhere else on his plan for Belvoir. The raised semi-circular Bowling Green that had been built here in the early 18th century on ancient foundations was to be removed: all 23,000 cubic yards of it, which very roughly converts to about 23,000 tons. Weirdly, it was so high up that it blocked light into half the lower floor windows, so it had to go. John Dodson & Company were contracted to dig it all out and transport it firstly in wheel barrows and later on gang wagons via temporary railways – as they did for the 'Subterranean Passage' in the Dooms – 50 yards or so down the hill, to build an embankment. The earthwork would link Castle Hill to Blackberry Hill and level out the very steep declivity between the two hills which must have made for a hazardous carriage ride.

Brown had proposed putting a tunnel through the embankment to provide quick access between the Woodland Gardens and Old Park on the northern perimeter, but it never happened. I wonder if Mr Worsdale's death in the Dooms in 1803 put paid to any suggestion of constructing another tunnel. However, to move the earth and build up the embankment took eight men an incredible two-and-a-half years, from December 1801 to May 1804. The digging went as far down as the bedrock, taking out all the cellars' foundations under and around the Bowling Green, and with it, most probably, Robert de Todeni's 11th-century motte. Peter Foden, our archivist, pointed out to me how hard it would have been for the poor Anglo-Saxons to take the earth up here in the first place without any engineering to help them. All this was going on in front of the old chapel, so it's perhaps no surprise that Dodson's men were tasked with demolishing that as well, along with the old picture gallery that stuck out at a 45° angle – colourfully described by Joseph Hill as 'an ugly Excrescence'.

Such an historic site is bound to hold secrets, even skeletons. In a letter from the 5th Duke to Elizabeth on 8th August, 1803, he wrote: '...I had nearly forgotten that in removing the earth from the site of the old chapel this morning the skeleton of a human body was found without any coffin, it must have laid there for centuries but the teeth were uncommonly perfect, and not one wanting.' He continued to explain that the Revd John

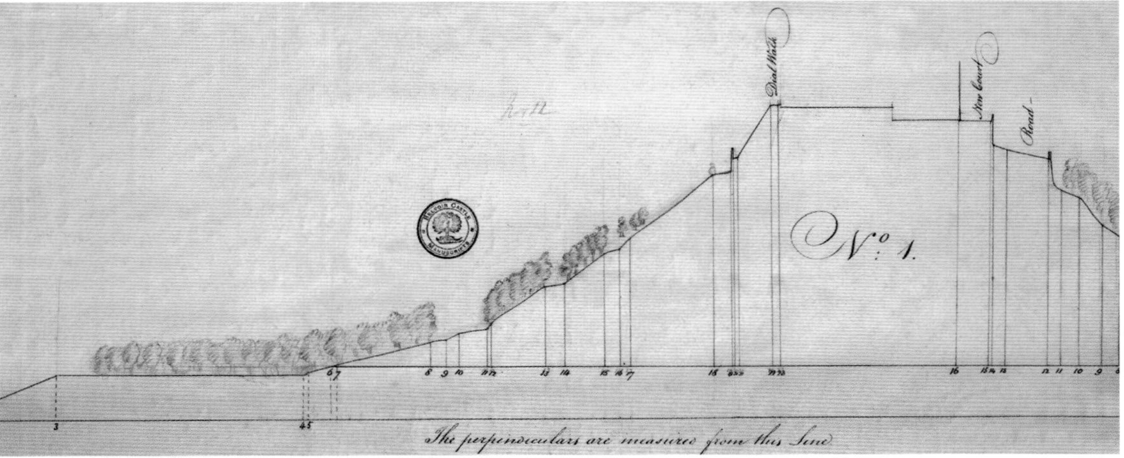

Thoroton had ordered it to be very carefully deposited in a box and committed again to the ground in roughly the same place as it had been found.

During our research into the gardens, we discovered that the front of the new chapel and the rest of the Castle's southwest elevation were not designed by James Wyatt as we had always believed, but chiefly by Frederick Trench who had based his work on Brown's plans. The information, discovered in a letter from Joseph Hill to the 4th Duke 10 days before the Duke's death, also gives credence to the ideas that the 4th Duke was very much in-tune with Brown's plans for Gothic Revival for both house and garden. Hill wrote: 'One of my principal Cares has been, to consider with Mr Thoroton, Mr Trench's Plans for the Improvement of the Castle. Your Grace is aware that Mr Brown's Plans have not been transmitted to Me – Mr Trench's Designs are agreed on all Hands to be very elegant; & if the Castle was to be rebuilt intirely from the Ground, his gothick Fronts would be extremely handsome.'

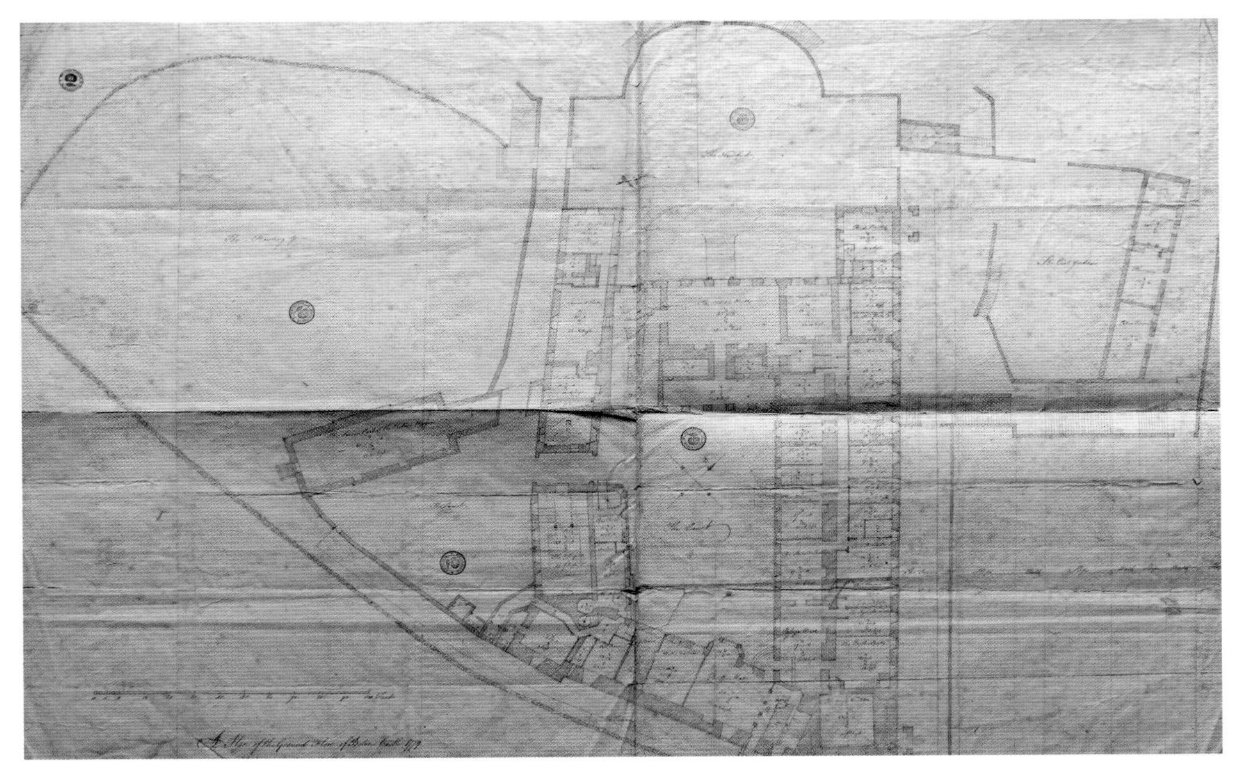

There are three plans in our archives of this Castle elevation: one is signed by Brown, another by Wyatt and a third was unsigned and assumed to be by Revd John Thoroton, but we now know that it was Frederick Trench's work. The only alteration to the plan appears to be Wyatt's extension of Trench's rotunda, which became the Round Tower (opposite). The letter also demonstrates the importance of the Trench family's architectural influence at Belvoir. Frederick Trench's son, Col Frederick Trench, was to become a close friend of Elizabeth's and together, with his friend, HRH The Duke of York, they would join forces to form a powerful triumvirate with architectural ambitions way beyond the confines of Belvoir.

PREVIOUS PAGES
AUTUMN ON THE 'MODERN' TERRACES

OPPOSITE (above)
THE ROUND TOWER is an icon of Belvoir's architecture and is Wyatt's extension of Trench's rotunda. In front is the Bowling Green (see opposite top)

OPPOSITE (below)
CROSS SECTION of Spiral Walk that was softened to create the embankment

LEFT (above)
1779 PLAN OF THE GROUND FLOOR, clearly showing the Bowling Green at the upper left

(below)
TRENCH'S FIRST PROPOSAL FOR THE SOUTH FRONT, with a Rotunda which Wyatt converted into the Round Tower and the Chapel with its twin towers, as illustrated by the photograph (opposite above)

ABOVE
EARLY 19th CENTURY LADY watering (Paris fashion plate)
Private Collection / The Stapleton Collection / Bridgeman Images

PETO'S ROSE GARDEN

This area is now the gentle grassy slope that Brown imagined, and it rolls down to the first of the terraces – the Rose Garden. This part of the garden has undergone several changes with most Duchesses leaving their mark. It was terraced in 1814 and Thoroton (now the Revd Sir John Thoroton after being knighted by the Prince Regent in 1813 for his architectural innovations), had 'plans and models' made of the 'Flower Gardens'[28] by Thomas Cochran in 1815. Thoroton, who was divorced, lived in the Castle and his rooms were in the tower that overlooked this part of the garden. I like to think that he took control of its development, although it does seem unlikely that Elizabeth would have given him an entirely free rein, except that they had great respect for each other.[29] Entries in the gardener's record books note several requests from Sir John to prune and one where he works with the pruners, so it's very likely that he had been managing the maintenance of the roses, at the very least.

[28] Belvoir Archives
[29] Ibid.

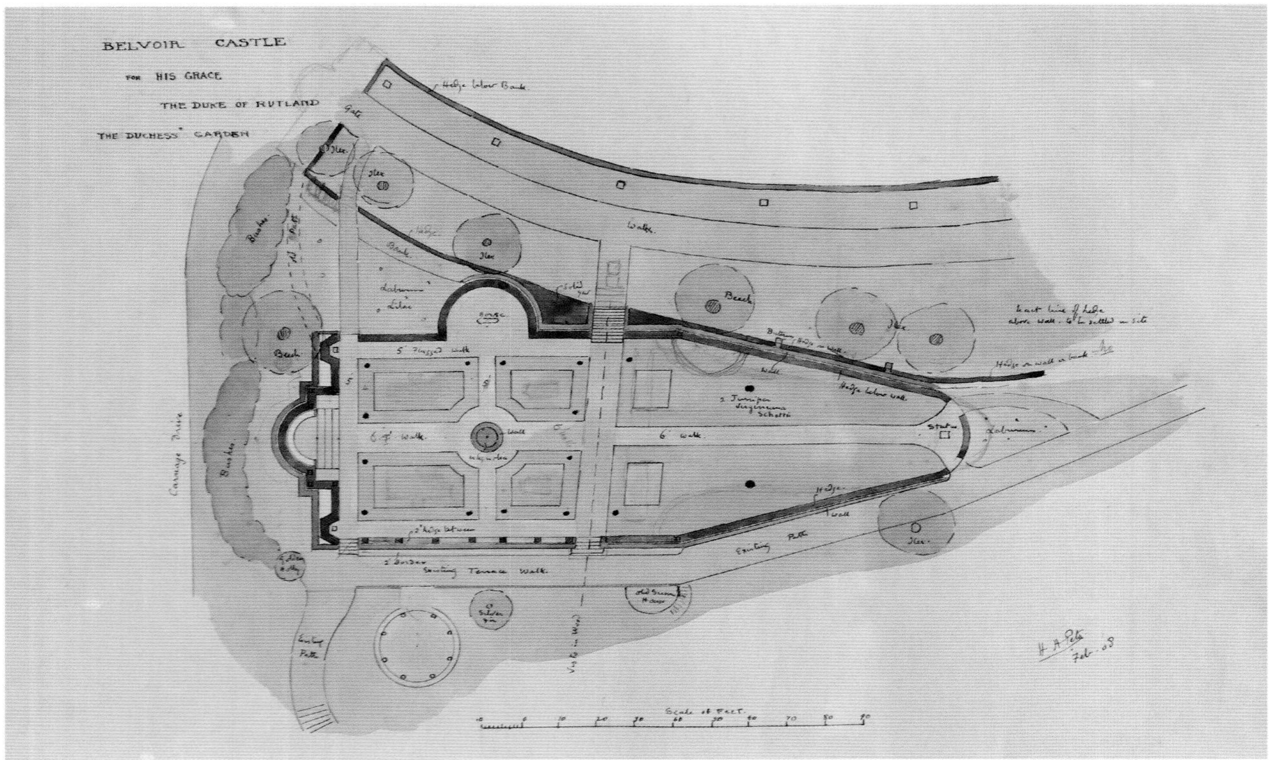

Not only was Thoroton an old family friend, he and Elizabeth shared an enthusiasm for architecture. He also saved the 5th Duke and Duchess's children from the fire in 1816 that destroyed so much of the new building work. When he died in 1820, Elizabeth wrote to her friend, Col Frederick Trench, clearly shaken with grief: 'I wander about...crying all the way I go, for everything I see recalls him to my imagination.'

One of the most striking features in this garden is Caius Gabriel Cibber's statue of Winter. A total of seven statues by Cibber were commissioned in 1680. The other six include Spring, Autumn and Summer; two statues represent the senses of smell and taste, and finally, Juno with her peacock insignia (from the Manners crest). They are all in the Statue Garden just below the Rose Garden. Cibber (1630-1700) was a talented Danish émigré who had settled in Grantham. He was a mason and sculptor of the highest calibre having collaborated with Sir Christopher Wren in London and was patronised by both Charles II and William III. The 1st Duke of Rutland (1638-1711) commissioned him to embellish the Spiral Walk to the third 'Castle' that his parents, the 8th Earl and Countess had built. The statues were carved in Ketton stone and, according to the original correspondence in the archives, the hefty price of £35 (circa £140,000) included placing the works in-situ and for: 'The Earl to find the said Cibber and his two workmen diett and

STATUE OF WINTER.

lodging at Bellvoyer whilest he workes upon the said statues.'

Fresh from completing a Grand Tour with her husband in 1814, Elizabeth soon decided to rearrange the statues and set them into the hillside: Winter residing over these two terraces and the others carefully positioned in Italian style in what became the Statue Garden. Stone steps and balustrades were made for them in August 1814. The next change came nearly 100 years later, in 1906, when Violet commissioned the distinguished landscape architect and lover of the Italian Renaissance, Harold Peto (1854-1933) to redesign the area – although she characteristically takes most of the credit for herself!

PART OF THE STATUARY GARDEN.

OPPOSITE (above)
FORMAL YEW HEDGES are a feature of the garden

OPPOSITE (below)
HAROLD PETO'S PLAN of 1906 for the garden we essentially see today

ABOVE AND TOP LEFT
STATUE OF WINTER and
PART OF THE STATUE GARDEN from Divers' book

LEFT
STATUE OF 'WINTER'

The gardener, Divers, makes a wonderfully dry comment in his book, *The Castle Flower Garden*: 'This is the name usually given to the triangular piece of ground by the side of the carriageway drive, near the Castle. Considerable alterations have been made there since these notes were first written.' I suspect that this was a guarded criticism of Violet who had casually obliterated Divers' precious Victorian flowerbeds planted with aubretia, tulips and rose arbours.

Violet also wrote about the Rose Garden in her notebook: 'It is approached by an old pair of iron gates. Yew hedges I put encircle all the top side. The lie of the Castle made it a very difficult question – a precipice taking its own line. Peto found the shape of the prow of a boat the best solution – a very high wall excavating and leveling was necessary to get it formal and interesting – and flagged paths, a half-circled seat raised on steps and a small lily pond.'

Together they made a straight vista from the first flight of steps, brought the stone statues of children from the Duchess's Garden and enclosed a circular stone seat with yew hedging. Violet had lion head brackets carved from an old plaster model found in the cellar of her London house at 16 Arlington Street. She wrote: 'I think it had been a model for some Console table for Belvoir – round the model in 18th cent: writing was This is the Duke of Rutlands.' She added: 'A very beautiful grass drive or walk ends just under my Rotunda – & at the end I have placed the other Urn – 2 more urns are by Queenie's seat on 3d Terrace South'. Queenie was her husband's half-sister. If only Violet had drawn diagrams to illustrate her notes, we could be certain which areas she refers to, but her passion remains compelling and is a great source of inspiration.

A Corinthian column, now adorned with creamy yellow roses, was bought in Bologna during a trip with her daughter, Diana, in 1907. Diana noted wryly: 'My mother, though limited to her hundred pounds, seemed to have '*carte blanche*' with the Belvoir Clerk of the Works, so she bought unstintingly...and Forum-sized marble pillars for her Italian garden at Belvoir.'[30] To her delight, Violet also discovered, hidden in overgrown shrubberies, the striking marble Chinese Monumental Horse that had been brought from India and presented in 1851 to the 5th Duke of Rutland by Admiral Thomas Cochrane. Against Peto's advice, Violet chose to position the horse in the perfect place, directly in the 'prow'. We still haven't found out who designed the planting plan but I expect Violet had a very strong hand in directing Divers.

OPPOSITE
SIGHTS AND SCENTS of the Rose Garden

RIGHT
THE PAVILION provides views of the Statue Garden

[30] Diana Cooper, *op. cit.*

Confidently, without Peto, she went on to cut out the deep terrace below the Statue Garden to make an inviting grass walk through bluebells with rhododendrons planted everywhere. She dreamed of placing a sculpted figure on the hill beyond, perhaps one by Harris Thorneycroft, but sadly this proved 'too expensive to contemplate'. [31]

In 2003, with my youngest child, Hugo still only a babe-in-arms, every corner of every garden at Belvoir needed work, but it was obvious that the Rose Garden was a priority. Without disturbing Peto's grand design we needed to replace a lot of very tired plants. The roses were also in a terrible state, which meant starting again not only with new plants but new soil.

With a very tight budget and little knowledge of planting, I rang the late Peter Beales, the well-known rose expert who exhibited at Chelsea Flower Show every year. He agreed to help in return for free marketing for his company. He was a lovely man and we had much fun creating the gardens together. Yellow roses are a favourite of David, the current Duke, and my late father-in-law, and they were a prerequisite to the success of the plan which, when it was finished, surpassed all our expectations.

THIS PAGE & OPPOSITE
THE CIBBER STATUES, commissioned for the 8th Earl of Rutland, date from 1680 and are some of the oldest in the country

[31] Violet's notebook

THE STATUE GARDEN

The Rose Garden descends steeply into the shaded Japanese Woodland via what used to be a grassy bank, carpeted with daffodils in the spring and, of course, the Cibber statues. Our head gardener at the time, Richard Jackson, had been working in a romantic garden in Norfolk before he worked for us and was keen to help me design a knot garden that would benefit from being seen from the Rose Garden above. We worked on a traditional design that would represent the current Duke and Duchess of Rutland with a design that included the initials of 'D' and 'E' for David and Emma.

We also wanted to dig out a pond as the area was extremely boggy. However, we managed to pick one of the wettest winters on record and when the digger got stuck, we had to rethink. Determined not to give up, we found some old Victorian stone steps and built the pond up, rather than digging down.

To my absolute astonishment, it was only when I later saw Peto's plans for the Rose Garden that we realised he had made provision for exactly the same design in the Statue Garden.

THE PRESENT DUKE'S & DUCHESS'S INITIALS
form the centrepieces of two mirrored parterres

A PERSPECTIVE VIEW OF BELVOIR CASTLE, IN THE
5
2
Engraved for the Universal Magazine, for J. Hinton at the Kings A

***A PERSPECTIVE VIEW OF BELVOIR CASTLE** c. 1750*

Mary Evans Picture Library

The *naïve* perspective of this mid-18th century engraving exaggerates the precipitate *glacis* propping up the Bowling Green, which partially obscured the ground floor windows of the Castle. It was this angular mountain of earth that was planed down to create Brown's embankment across the valley below in 1801-4

See also, in their original location, Caius Cibber's 1680 statues that gave the *Image Walk* its name and which still enjoy pride of place in the Statue Gardens

THE PET CEMETERY

Leading down again, through an arched laburnum walk is the compact 130m^2 pet cemetery enclosed by a beech hedge, tucked into Brown's embankment. How I remember our first burial with the Revd Stuart Foster officiating and all the house staff in attendance. Pagan, our ancient and beloved chocolate labrador had passed away and Horton, our then butler, led a small procession of weeping children to his final resting place in the corner of this fabulous garden. Sadly, more beloved dogs and cats have since been buried in this beautiful resting place.

We planted a yew hedge on the bank behind the fabulously ornamental bench that Violet fashioned from weathered stone carvings. The Rutland coat of arms, with 1666 dated on the stone, is believed to have been above the front door of the third Castle. Violet's garden was very different to ours: '...there used to be a bit of a Rustic Pergola where 4 roads paths met – but it all fell in one winter & no one regretted it – I then caused a Rotunda to be made with a path through it and a seat with teak seats in the upper side & steps mounting decorated by old Coats of arms – There is nothing placed in the middle of my Circle – because I saw young Children & Schoolroom girls acting Comedies & tragedies – on the outer side of the Circle – while we would sit on the upper side of the Circle'.

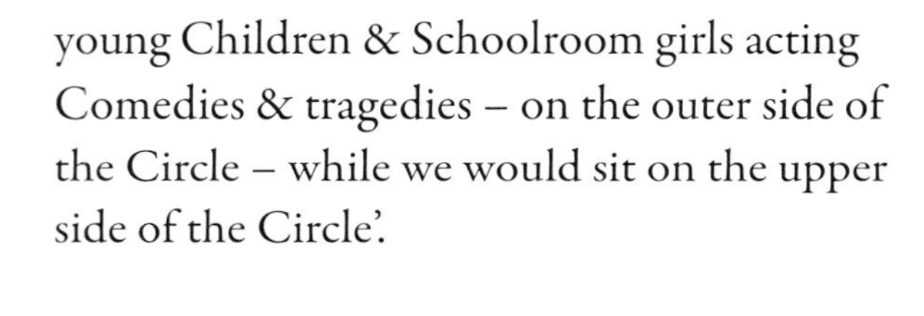

Now that the hedges have matured, and the cemetery garden is enclosed, it feels like a very special and spiritual place. As the gardens drop away again into the woodland garden, the palm trees, planted over 100 years ago, are a little unusual in a garden in the Midlands. They are reminders of the versatility of our soil type and position on the south-facing hill. Gardening in wet, boggy ground at the bottom of this terrace was a steep learning curve. Brown had been an expert in drainage of course, and the 4th Duke's agent, Joseph Hill, had employed Joseph Elkington, one of the best drainage experts in the business at the time. I could fully understand why. The area at the bottom of the Statue Garden was rumoured to have had a stream running through it once, although no one could remember when. It had so many boggy areas that I was going to need expert help to transform it into the beautiful Japanese Woodland that it is now.

LEFT
BEYOND THE NEW CIRCULAR POND
embedded with statues, is the exotic Japanese Woodland

OPPOSITE
1666 IS CARVED INTO THE STONE RUTLAND COAT OF ARMS
that is believed to have once been above the door of the third Castle

PAGAN
LIVER LABRADOR
FEB 1992 - 11TH FEB 2006
PERKY
GREY CAT
MAY 1997 - 17TH JUNE 2005
BELOVED FRIENDS TO
THE MANNERS FAMILY
WE DO MISS YOU
BOTH SO MUCH
POPPY

CHAPTER FIVE

THE JAPANESE WOODLAND

This garden in Priory Hole Wood is positioned just underneath Brown's embankment, which, as I have already mentioned, was built using roughly 23,000 tons of earth from the old Bowling Green, 100 yards up the hill. It would have been an obvious idea to dump the earth in the bottom of the very steep and awkward declivity between Castle Hill, which the Castle sits on, and Blackberry Hill. Brown had wanted to bring his main driveway in from Harston, over Blackberry Hill and up to the Castle but such a steep ravine would have been torturous for carriages, especially in icy conditions. It would also have crossed the old Redmile to Woolsthorpe public road (which possibly originated from an ancient Roman road)[32] running in a west-east direction along the valley floor. It was diverted in 1734 but was still used as a shortcut by many locals. Spyers had shown a clump of trees on his 'before' drawings but they can't have been dense enough to deter all trespassers and probably poachers, too. You can imagine the fun Brown would have had when he hit on the idea to block the road for good with a 30ft high wall of earth.

Today, traffic leaves the Castle in a southerly direction along the top of Brown's embankment before turning east on to the one-way drive that cuts through Priory Hole Wood, with the new Japanese Woodland on the left. It's named as such because of the Japanese and Chinese plants used here, not because it's full of pagodas and oriental ornaments, which I understand has confused some visitors. Somewhere between the drive and the Duke's Walk higher up the hill is the location for the first grotto, Merlin's Cave, recorded at Belvoir. Spyers marked it and two others on his survey. There is no trace of any of them now, and nobody knows anything about them or what happened to them, except that they were likely to have been built for John of the Hill. When we first looked at this area, and I use the word 'area' carefully, it was a mass of overgrowth – brambles, weeds, thorn, you name it – under a beautiful canopy of oaks. Clearing was obviously going to be a priority but I needed a plan and help. After many discussions with gardeners and experts, I met an exhibitor at the Chelsea Flower Show in 2004 who understood exactly what we needed.

Charles Williams is the current owner of Burncoose Nurseries at his family's estate at Caerhays Castle in Cornwall. It has been owned by the Williams family since 1860 and has played an important part in the

[32] Recent surveys have suggested that the line of the old public road could have originated from a Roman road running from The Drift (a Roman road to the east) towards Margidunum through Belvoir and Redmile. Though the line is tentative, its close association with a possible Romano-British settlement on Blackberry Hill adds some weight to the claims

development of English gardening and horticulture. J. C. Williams (1861-1939) was one of the key sponsors and financiers of plant hunting expeditions to Western China by Ernest Wilson and George Forrest. They brought back seeds of literally thousands of species of plants and lots of them went first to Caerhays. Many of the magnolias, rhododendrons and camellias which thrive in Charles' 150-year-old woodland garden at his home are from that original seed collection.

Our Japanese Woodland is sheltered from north, east and westerly winds and the soil is rich and broadly ericaceous. Plus there are plenty of wet patches ensuring plants don't dry out in hot summers. The area is perfect for rhododendrons and camellias that work so well in woodland gardens.

These days, we think nothing of planting species from all over the world such is the access to seeds. It's easy to forget that in 1831 Belvoir's garden was once considered to be one of the greatest gardens north of London, along with Trentham and Chatsworth, specifically because of its limited use of newly imported exotic plants.[33] Certainly none of these Chinese plants were available in Brown's time, and I wonder how he would have used them if he'd had the opportunity.

So, work began with a rigorous clearance programme and a heavy felling of nearly half of the existing tree cover to give the dapple sunlight effect that camellias need to succeed in the ericaceous soil. It requires a leap of faith to chop down so many trees, until you realise it's all been done before. In a letter to the 4th Duke, Hill wrote: 'The Oaks in Priors Hole ought to have been thind long ago – If Your Grace will permit some of the Trees to be taken down under the direction of some skilful Person the Trees that remain will be much benefited by it.'[34]

Our plan was to design a woodland garden with long distance views and vistas whereby visitors could catch a glimpse of a tree magnolia in flower or the autumn colour of a Japanese acer from afar. Woodland gardens are not intended to be seen all at once, but enjoyed from different angles and perspectives that change through the year. The idea was to create maximum impact from the Castle and along the descent to James Wyatt's Dairy at the bottom of this garden.

PREVIOUS PAGE AND OPPOSITE
HYDRANGEAS AND RHODODENDRONS work so well by lengthening the flowering window

RIGHT
AZALEA 'ROYAL COMMAND'

[33] First commented on in print by Alexander Gordon during the 5th Duke's time, when Mr Buckwell was the head gardener in 1831
[34] Belvoir Archives

On our regular walks into the gardens we check over the 100 specimen camellias that were planted in 2006. Another 150 were planted in 2014. As well as camellias we have planted tree magnolias, specimen hydrangeas, azaleas and rhododendrons, snake-bark and Japanese maples and various bamboos.

On one walk with my youngest daughter, Eliza, we noticed the ground was particularly wet in several places, and the old rumours of a stream trickling along the valley floor surfaced again. We could see that this area had the potential to become another magnificent walk, but with mud oozing way over our ankles, it was obvious we had to take some drastic measures. I booked a driver in a JCB and we held our breath in case it sank, as it had in the Statue Garden, but to our relief it held firm. So, we dug one pond and then we dug another, and called them Eliza's Ponds. They have given this garden tranquil breathing space and a sense of balance between the planting schemes, as well as becoming another draw for wildlife – the local herons love them – and a focal point at the back of the Dairy.

While all the grubbing, clearing and planting was going on, we discovered what appeared to be an old pathway snaking through the garden from the bottom of the Statue Garden that stretched to the drive. It was an exciting day when we discovered the path continued over the tarmac and up through the woods to the Duchess's Gardens. The Revd Irwin Eller, author of *The History of Belvoir Castle, From the Norman Conquest to The Nineteenth Century,* wrote in 1841: 'The Duchess' Garden was reached along narrow walks through 'a kind of wilderness,' and this must be the narrow walk. Suddenly, all these island gardens had a link and it spurred us all on to restore the pathways and the rest of the gardens. Violet had described it in her notebook: [from] 'the statue garden – which goes very deep in the Valley before it mounts in an inviting grass walk (in Spring covered with bluebells) to the high hill & beyond – an avenue ending in the highest oaks.'

Restoring the walk has been a real journey of discovery for me; I've learnt so much about woodland gardening but the real excitement has been to understand Elizabeth's vision for a contemporary garden within Brown's mediaeval backdrop, and how the two work so well together.

There are still parallels with her methods today. Charles Williams took great pains to work with the forestry team. Woodland gardeners have very different ideas to foresters, which I recently discovered when we realised that Elizabeth employed her head woodman to oversee her woodland gardens and her head gardener to tend to the flower gardens on the terraces and the kitchen garden.

In woodland gardens, tree stumps and serried ranks of new planting are not allowed. The strimming has to be so careful so as not to damage tender bark on young trees. Wild flower meadows have to be strimmed in July after they have seeded and died back, and done again in October to control the brambles. The big-hitting weeds like burdock, ragwort, nettles and docks need special attention so they don't kill off the seedling foxgloves which will give plenty of colour while the new planting becomes established. The whole process is similar to forestry work, but with a much lighter hand.

OPPOSITE (left)
RHODODENDRON with Japanese pergola behind

OPPOSITE (right)
CAMELLIAS AND NARCISSI above the Pet Cemetery

LEFT
AZALEA 'ROYAL COMMAND' in the foreground, looking towards the Statue Garden

Woodland trees and specimen trees now all work together in harmony. The tallest cherry trees (*Prunus avium*) in the British Isles are among the beeches, sycamore, Holm oaks and tulip trees on this walk. Elizabeth is credited for choosing cherry, yew and oak here, adding to the feeling of a natural landscape. Trees were her passion, and especially oak. In a letter to her husband dated September 1805, she wrote: 'Before I take leave of my favourite subject I must tell you I was to hear that you intend to plant on different parts of your estate, it will be doing your country good in times to come, as oak timber will I hear grow scarce and if that should happen we are undone as a nation.' Oaks have always been a national symbol of strength and survival, and have played an important part in English folklore. Up until the mid-19th century, oak was the primary material for shipbuilding, which is probably why Elizabeth prized her oaks so much given that the country was in the middle of the Napoleonic Wars.

OPPOSITE
JAPANESE WOODLAND
in late summer

RIGHT (above)
WOVEN WILLOW STAG
with real antlers by Laury Dizengremel, looks over Eliza's Pond

RIGHT (below)
DAFFODILS COMBINE WITH PALMS
during early spring

OVER
WOVEN WILLOW SCULPTURE
of a mythical Welsh dragon, by Laury Dizengremel, reflects the present Duchess's country of birth

CHAPTER SIX

THE DUCHESS'S GARDEN

This is the four-acre garden that my mother-in-law, Frances, the Dowager Duchess of Rutland, rediscovered in 1970 when she forced open the rusty gate on a walk with her young children. Within hours she was back with a scythe and began the meticulous task of restoring Belvoir's iconic Spring Gardens (Duchess's and Hermit's Gardens) that had been neglected for 30 years since the Second World War. It must have been a daunting prospect; it wasn't just three decades of overgrowth to deal with but there was the added pressure of taking on a garden that had been famous twice: once as one of the finest examples of a Picturesque garden in the Regency period and later for spring bedding during the Victorian era. A great deal of the present planting is down to Frances' skills as a very accomplished plantswoman and gardener.

Before Brown considered its capabilities in 1780, it was a wooded hillside, known as Gorsey Close,[35] later known as Briery Hill Woods and oozing with several natural springs.[36] Records show large-scale felling taking place between 1790-1793 and quarrying in 1791 that has left the area with small scoops and hollows. One detects the work of Joseph Hill here to raise money after the 4th Duke had allowed him to 'rescue' the estate from bankruptcy in the 1780s.

Brown made provision for a 'shady seat' in this wooded pleasure garden. But Elizabeth wanted more than just a shady seat. She wanted a secret garden to be discovered after a walk through natural woodland. Lewis Kennedy, of Lee and Kennedy, the top nursery in the world at the time,[37] drew designs for a secret garden at Wrotham Park (another estate where Brown visited and proposed plans, but nothing started on it until the 1820s). They are a good example of the type, though nothing like the scale of this garden. Lee and Kennedy supplied plants to Belvoir from at least 1807-1820s and it's quite possible that Lewis' son, John Kennedy, would have advised Elizabeth. Not only was he a leading nurseryman, he was also one of the three or four best landscape gardeners of the day.

The Ladies Garden, as it was originally referred to, was started in 1814. Elizabeth had just lost a little boy – George – at less than a year old. The project must have helped

[35] Gorsey Close was an ancient enclosure of pasture belonging to the Knipton Manor House we now know as Knipton Lodge
[36] Spyers' survey, 1779
[37] John Claudius Loudon described Lee and Kennedy in 1854 as: 'For many years this nursery was deservedly considered the first in the world.' Loudon, *Arboretum et fruiticetum britannicum*, 1854

her with her grief (she had already lost a daughter and another son), as well as giving her a place to escape to because the Castle was still under construction. Work on the Duke's Walk (a two-mile circuitous walk around the Pleasure Ground) had been going on for a few years and a seat and steps were being made for it only a year before. After that, work appears to have gained real momentum with William Shill leading his woodland team and transporting sods and gravel to the site while Elizabeth's gardeners planted both common and Portuguese laurels along the walks. Seats were an essential requirement for the garden and the first entry in the Ledgers, dated August 1816, records: '*altering the area of the duchess's seat*', which suggests significant time and attention were taken to ensure it was just right. There are constant entries for more seats in the Ladies Garden and Duke's Walk until August 1818 when there is an entry to '*making the Pavilion*'. No Picturesque garden was complete without pavilions and grottos and this garden acquired several of both, some of which still exist. If you had to choose only one place for a seat, it would be where the fabulous Root and Moss house (or summer house, as it's also referred to) is now.

By 1819, the roof was stripped and replaced with thatched reed, which took 22 days to complete at a cost of £7:14:0. (£510 in today's money). The cost of the carriage of the reeds cost over three times as much. When it was re-thatched and restored in 2014, it cost £20,000 which included woodworm treatment – something that wouldn't have been considered in the early 19th century. It sits very comfortably above a series of stone steps commanding an unrivalled vista through trees and shrubs to a new pond with an elegant statue; then on to the lake and up again to Brown's perimeter tree belt at Woolsthorpe and Harston Hill.

The current Duke's aunt, Lady Ursula D'Abo – known as Aunt Ursie – can remember sitting in it in 1925 with her 73-year-old grandfather (the 8th Duke). She would have been nine when she trotted alongside Appa, as she called him, in his chair being wheeled from the Castle to the Duke's Walk by his nurse, Sister Malone, where they would sit together in the Root and Moss House.

OPPOSITE
THE ROOT AND MOSS HOUSE, built in 1818 and restored in 2014

LEFT
VIEW FROM THE DUKE'S WALK, approaching the Root and Moss House through the gardens

She recalls: 'The view below embraced spreading gardens and gravel walks and a huge wood leading to the main drive. The gardens were beautifully kept with terraces of flowers and shrubs and specimen trees and – it has always stuck in the memory – an extraordinary monkey puzzle tree. I loved the scented azaleas and the rhododendrons, under which convenient benches nestled at the top of stone steps flanked with stone urns. It was a truly romantic English garden.'[38]

The monkey puzzle tree (*Araucaria araucana)* was planted in the place where Brown had planned a focal point to rise above the tree canopy. It was to have been viewed from the Castle terraces and as visitors approached from the other side of the valley. For a lot of people, you either love these trees or hate them, but I have a huge fondness for it and its character casts a wonderfully light-hearted feel to this garden. It's not without some fame of its own, either. Divers wrote in his book that the tree was planted in 1842, which makes it one of the first grown in the country. William Lobb, employed by the famous seed producers, Veitch, only sent the seed back from South America around 1841/2. Veitch weren't officially selling seedlings (at £10 per 100) before 1843, so someone must have been using their contacts, or it could have been a gift.

[38] Lady Ursula d'Abo, *The Girl with the Widow's Peak*, 2014

One other tree that incites comment is the Viagra tree, at least that is what we call it. The bark is meant to have similar properties to a Viagra tablet – not that anyone has tried it, but it's a good story. Its official name is *Cercidiphyllum japonica* and it is also known as the Katsura tree. It has beautiful heart-shaped leaves that turn a glorious orange red in the autumn. When the leaves start to fall it has a strong smell of caramel; if you stand underneath it and close your eyes, you would really think you were in a sweet shop.

Looking at this garden now is a source of enormous pride to me and to the whole team of gardeners who have worked on the massive restoration. The inspiration came from Charles Williams, who created a similar large woodland garden at Caerhays. But working in this garden is not for the faint-hearted. The steepness of the banks and the many wet patches from the springs make it not only impossible to mow with a conventional lawnmower, but you can't even push a wheelbarrow up and down. Horses must have dragged the huge boulders in here during Elizabeth's time. We could have done with horses when our gardeners, Martin and Nikki, rebuilt the rockery. After a couple of days of torrential rain the ground was too wet to walk up hill, but they only had the digger for one day and they had to get on with transporting new rocks into place. The mess was indescribable but the results are fantastic and rewarding for all of us.

DOUBLE ARABIS AND TULIPS.

OPPOSITE
THE MONKEY PUZZLE TREE is believed to be one of the first to be planted in the country in 1842

TOP LEFT
THE SMOKE BUSH 'ROYAL PURPLE' (*Cotinus coggygria*) creates a wonderful contrast with the the Katsura tree (*Cercidiphyllum japonica*) otherwise known to us as the 'Viagra tree'

BELOW (left)
A VIEW OF THE VICTORIAN BEDDING from the top of the steps, circa 1909

BELOW (right)
***TAXODIUM DISTICHUM* – its striking rust colour is a highlight of autumn**

FLOWER BEDS IN THE DUCHESS' GARDEN.

Rogue sycamores, ash, brambles and nettles have been cleared along the bowl of the amphitheatre while others have been thinned, cut back and replaced. We have planted cuttings from the rice paper tree on the terrace gardens; over 250 new, rare and unusual acid loving trees and plants were planted in 2012 and with the excellent wet summer that followed in 2013, they are establishing nicely. We rebuilt the rockery with large stones imported from Belvoir Castle's own quarry, some weighing over three to four tons each, and planted it up with many of the flora that Divers had so enthused about in his rockery.

Elizabeth's spirit feels very much alive in this garden, and while we were working on all the improvements I really wanted to create our own fitting tribute to her memory. Inspiration came from the wonderful portrait of her in

OPPOSITE (left)
CLASSICAL SCULPTURE found on the estate. Strongly resembling Elizabeth, it now stands in her garden

OPPOSITE (right)
THE VICTORIAN SPRING FLOWERING BEDS in the Duchess's Garden, *c.* 1909

LEFT
ELIZABETH, 5th DUCHESS (1780-1825) by John Hoppner

MIDDLE
EMMA in similar pose next to the original column

One cultivated spot behold which spread
Its flowery bosom of the moontide beam
Where numerous rosebuds near their blending heads
And poppies gay and fragrant vi'lets team.

Far from the busy world's unceasing sound
Here has Eliza fix'd her favourite seat
Chaste emblems of the tranquil scene around
Pure as the flowers that smile beneath her feet.

Poem inscribed on the column

the ballroom by John Hoppner (1758-1810). She is painted as if leaning against the column which now stands in the centre of this garden, and close to the Moss and Root House, looking down the steps close to a pond.

The stone column has survived exactly where it's shown in the painting but the original pond is long gone. At the same time as renovating this part of the garden, we were making improvements to one of the rented properties on the Estate and we came across a rather beautiful statue that looked very much like the young Elizabeth. So the two ideas came together and we built a new, natural shaped pond with the statue in the middle. Now, when you look from the Moss and Root House your eye takes you straight to 'Elizabeth' and the pond that is shown to her left in her picture.

Brown had envisaged an open amphitheatre of verdant 'lawn', edged most probably with beds and borders of the Duchess's choice. The lawn idea strikes me as odd as the slope is far too steep and inaccessible to mow. Today we strim it but, back in Elizabeth's day, the gardeners would have had to cut the grass with scythes. No other gardeners could have achieved more with the formal Victorian ideals of bedding than Ingram and Divers, albeit over half a century after the plan had been drawn up and garden fashion was very different. William Ingram developed the Duchess's Gardens in the 1870s. His planting conformed to Gothic Revival and a return to the mediaeval style that Brown had favoured as a pure and English form of design.

Today, with only two part-time gardeners and occasional volunteers, the planting has reverted back to a style far more to Elizabeth's liking and the Picturesque, with swathes of camellias, azaleas and rhododendrons sharing the limelight with the earlier flowering drifts of naturalised daffodils, primroses and bluebells.

LEFT
THIS GHENT HYBRID AZALEA is one of the oldest in the gardens

OPPOSITE (left)
LACECAP and MOPHEAD HYDRANGEAS

CLOCKWISE (from top left)
ANTHEMIS, RHODODENDRON, THE HANDKERCHIEF TREE (*Davidia involucrata*), MEADOW SAGE (*Salvia pratensis* 'Indigo'), RICE PAPER TREE (*Tetrapanax papyrifer*), BEARDED IRIS 'Dusky Challenger', CROCOSMIA 'LUCIFER', WILLOW PEACOCK SCULPTURE

OVER
(left) **AUTUMN LEAVES (*Sorbus sargentiana*),** (right) **THE RED KITE (*Milvus milvus*) is one of our most spectacular birds,** (opposite) **a bird's eye view of the Hermit's Garden**

And we've had some fun with the statue of the 'Welsh dragon' made out of living willow. Laury Dizengremel is an artist I met several years ago and she has since moved to a cottage on the Estate and is our artist in residence. Her style works so well in the woodland and gives a 21st-century edge: a very satisfying nod to the evolution of a 200-year-old garden. After the bulbs comes a stunning display of ornamental trees from China, Japan and New Zealand; acers, bamboos, dogwoods, and cypress to create a dense patchwork of eye-catching bark and foliage. And that's where we might have stopped the restoration but, after discovering the footpath from the Japanese garden into the bottom of the Duchess's Garden, it was hard to resist carrying on with the theme.

CHAPTER SEVEN

THE HERMIT'S GARDEN

This seven-acre area adjoining the Duchess's Garden, like everywhere else in these gardens, had become choked with overgrowth. But it had very definite capabilities. Charles Williams, who had done so much to bring the woodland and Duke's Walk back to life, advised me to see the long-term potential in creating something that could inspire gardeners and non-gardening visitors alike. It sounded expensive, but he convinced me that if we could establish a collection of different and exciting plants that were rare and endangered in the wild, it would be quite a significant visitor experience and a great honour for us to be able to have all these amazing plants at Belvoir. It might also mean that, one day, we could merit National Collection status from Plant Heritage. And so his plans became reality as all sorts of weird and wonderful plants started to arrive, including over 50 magnolias. We also ordered many unusual *Enkianthus, Cornus, Stachyurus* and *Styrax* from different hemispheres, specifically to puzzle future generations and intrigue the experts with mature trees which are little known or appreciated in standard horticulture.

Clearance began in February, 2014. We started at the bottom of the Duchess's Garden and worked southwards. The job list was not for the lily-livered. Our gardeners, Nikki and Martin, with the help of Phil Burtt, removed virtually all the self-seeded sycamore, ash, elder, ponticum, laurel, box and sweet cherry, and all the declining older oaks. We left the yew, healthy oaks, coastal redwood (*Sequoia sempervirens)* and sweet chestnuts. Charles gave us strict instructions not to allow stumps and roots to be left in, as happens in forestry work, but to grub it all out properly to prevent honey fungus spreading. Bonfires were set on the paths in limited areas so as not to sterilise the soil, which makes planting impossible. It was literally a baptism of fire, for me. I had no idea clearing an area of overgrowth was so complicated.

With the site cleared, smoothed level and with no traces of debris, it was ready for planting. Charles and his nursery manager, Andrew Mills, arrived one horribly damp, foggy morning in March and, together with Martin and Nikki, placed out over 700 trees and shrubs. It took three weeks to get all these dug in, supported, and individually fenced to prevent deer and rabbit damage. Paths and edging continued and, by the end of April, three-quarters of the work was finished. The final 300 plants were planted in March 2015.

OPPOSITE
Nikki Applewhite (far left) and Charles Williams (centre) with a team of helpers begin the daunting task of planting the Hermit's Garden with 700 trees and shrubs

ABOVE
THE DUCHESS'S GARDEN
from the Hermit's Garden

OPPOSITE
THE TUFA GROTTO
was discovered during the restoration programme. It was built as a hermitage – an essential requirement in any Picturesque garden

While we were deciding what to call this 'new' garden, we had started work to uncover a couple of Regency grottos that were partly buried under overgrowth. Many estates in the late Georgian / early Victorian period paid a hermit to live in their grottos as a sort of novelty for visitors who walked past them – they were the ultimate ornament of a Picturesque landscape. The grotto would then have been called a hermitage, which literally means 'dwelling of a hermit'. We haven't been able to prove that our grottos were ever lived in, but it sounds romantic to call this the Hermit's Garden.

The first grotto we came across is made of exquisite tufa rock, a centuries-old material that develops when calcium-rich waters flow over organic material: twigs, leaves, moss and snail shells. As it dries out over time, the delicate organic material calcifies and it looks like coral. The gardeners had to carefully peel away decades of overgrowth so as not to damage it. Now you can see it properly, it does look as though a hermit could have lived in it – just. An old iron-railing gate opens into a roughly circular area that is no more than 12 feet across. A circular opening in the roof would have allowed smoke from a fire to escape, but it would have been very cramped. I have visions of a tiny, grey-bearded goblin reaching out through the gate to scare unwitting passers-by. In the absence of any evidence of a real hermit ever living in our tufa grotto, we commissioned Laury to

weave her magic and sculpt the shroud-like figure of a latter-day hermit that huddles outside the door.

Tufa grottos were popular in the 18th and 19th centuries; there is one at Croome Park in Worcestershire, the house and landscape that Brown had worked on for over 30 years. By coincidence, he built it not long after he had finished his Belvoir plans. It's a nice idea to imagine that he could have been thinking about Belvoir at the time, but it's more likely that he was inspired by the 'grotto of love' at Hampton Court when he suggested a grotto to Croome Park's owner, his old friend the Earl of Coventry and his second wife. The tufa for our grotto was delivered in the summer of 1822 and George Berrisford built it. Payment was also made to, 'R Shipman for Ale per Bill for unloading the Boats and getting the tufa down to the Grotto.' It would have been thirsty work.

OPPOSITE
THE GARDENER'S COSTUME
illustration from the *Dictionnaire des Sciences*, Denis Diderot (1713-84), c.1770 (engraving)

Private Collection / The Stapleton Collection / Bridgeman Images

LEFT (above)
A HERMIT'S VIEW
from the cave entrance. The view of the Castle is now obliterated by trees

LEFT (below)
BELVOIR CASTLE
from the HERMITAGE on the DUKE'S WALK, Col Frederick Trench, 1819

In complete contrast, the next grotto we found, 30 yards further along the Duke's Walk, is quite bland compared to the delicacy of the tufa. We think this building is 'Lord Granby's Cave' which, according to the Ledgers was roofed with glazed pantiles in 1830. It's easy to imagine Charles, the 5th Duke's son and heir, known as Lord Granby, and his two younger brothers coming here to play. Their poor mother, Elizabeth, would have been dead for five years and it may well have been somewhere they could escape from their four much older sisters.

The next leg of my tour is along the Duke's Walk to Frog Hollow, which takes in some spectacular scenery across the lakes to Woolsthorpe and Harston.

RIGHT (above)
CHARLES MANNERS, Marquis of Granby (later 6th Duke of Rutland), (1815-1888), Sir Francis Grant

RIGHT (below)
'LORD GRANBY'S CAVE' built for Elizabeth's boys after her death

OPPOSITE
EMMY SHELTON, volunteer gardener, tending new planting in the Hermit's Garden: including a young acer, June 2015

THE DUKE'S WALK

The two-mile circuitous Duke's Walk from the Castle began, in some form, in the mid-18th century and was developed fully for the 5th Duke and Duchess by 1816. Brown intended it to have regular 'diversions' or points of interest such as the one he planned at Wotton in Buckinghamshire for William Pitt the Elder. At each point, Brown may have verbally proposed a folly, or a bench or a small flower garden. It was also likely to have a carefully composed view of distinct quality. The route would have been varied with changing kinds of planting; evergreens, open grassy glades and woodland gardens. One striking feature of the whole walk is that it is pretty much entirely lined with box, holly, laurel, rhododendrons and yew. After every few yards there are patches of snowdrops in the winter, daffodils and bluebells in spring. It feels very much like a garden walk rather than a walk through woods.

OPPOSITE
AZALEAS between the Duchess's Garden and the Hermit's Garden, next to the Duke's Walk

ABOVE LEFT
THE DUKE'S WALK features notable trees such as an ancient yew, reputedly the tallest in Europe

LEFT
WOTTON HOUSE, Buckinghamshire

RIGHT
SNOWDROPS AND DAFFODILS intertwine spectacularly with the woodland

We have been restoring the edging on the walk and clearing out years of self-sown trees and unhealthy wood. The digger has been deployed to clear areas where the paths were lost entirely to neglect. Unfortunately, when you start digging out old tree roots on a slope you have to be careful not to start a landslide, which is exactly what happened to a 60-foot chunk of the walk above Knipton Pasture. We had had several days of heavy rain and the bank just slumped into the trees below. The cost of rebuilding it and strengthening it with boulders was an expense that hadn't been budgeted for and it slowed us down, but it's now safer than it's ever been and, after all the troubles, it's highly valued.

ABOVE
THE LANDSLIP
on the Duke's Walk

RIGHT
WOODLAND carpeted with ferns

OPPOSITE
AUTUMN provides a burst of colour at many points along the walk

CHAPTER EIGHT

FROG HOLLOW

On Brown's finished plan, Frog Hollow is identified as a deep, single valley hugging a skinny stream between Windsor Hill and Blackberry Hill, and appears to be roughly half the size it is now. He had proposed his perimeter belt of trees, complete with a riding, to be continued from Old Park Wood to the north of Knipton which effectively sliced through half the area we know today. Other than a few clumps of trees to soften the perimeter planting, there is no specific ornamentation.

The design would have been very attractive to look at from Brown's proposed drive from Harston had it been built. He'd deployed a similar feature on Spring Bank at Trentham, in Staffordshire. According to the Ledgers, it is likely that nothing was started in this far western corner of the plan until 1794. Four years later a road, or probably a track by today's standards, was built through Windsor Hill to Granby Wood. But it's likely that Elizabeth's interest in the site was stimulated when the public road, from Knipton to Redmile that runs along the top of Windsor Hill, was built in 1803. It exposed the whole valley giving a much wider space to develop than the area Brown had marked.

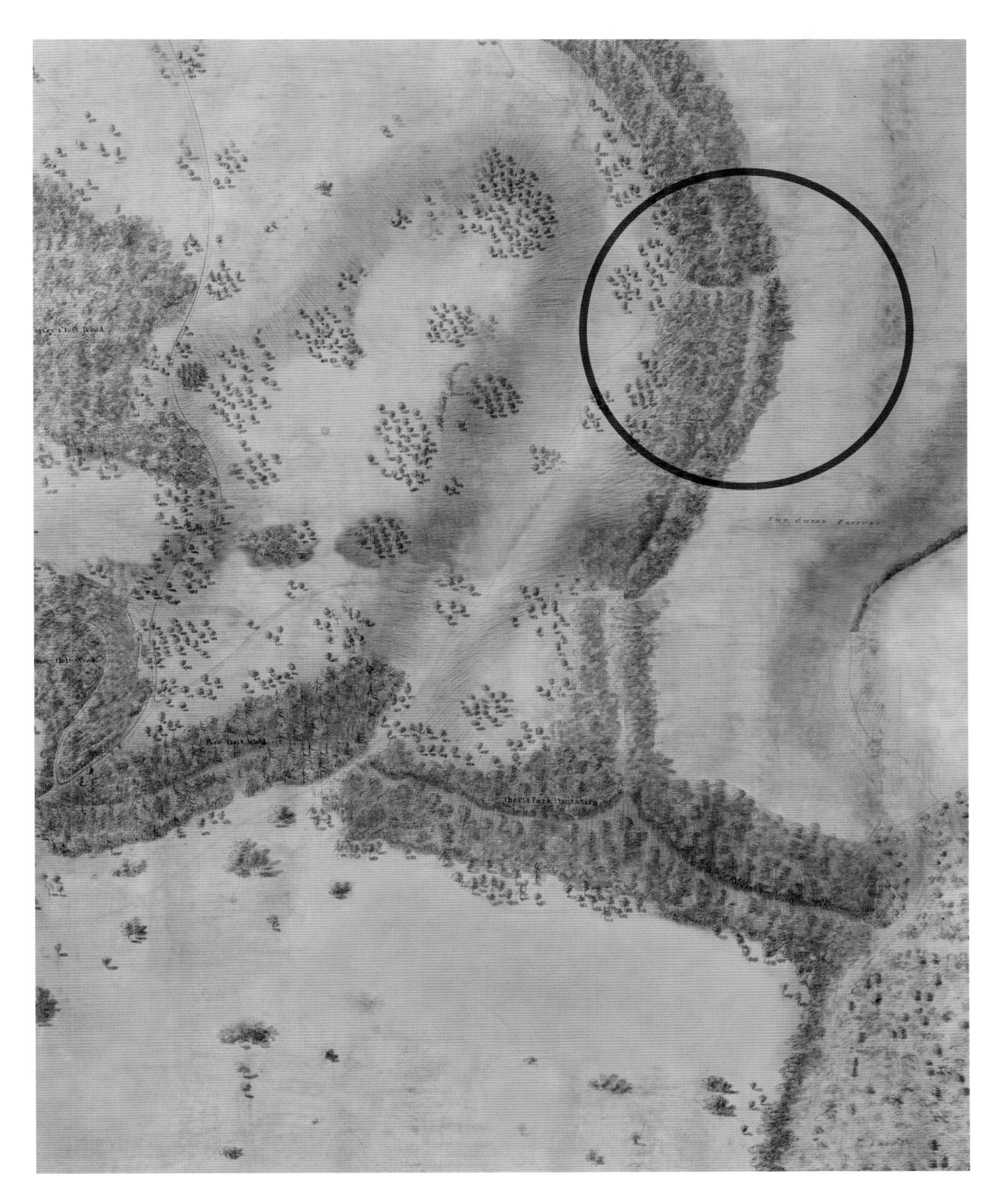

We know plants were being purchased at that time from Lee and Kennedy, the nurserymen to the Estate, for an American bog garden but we don't know where this garden was. There were many boggy places in the Pleasure Grounds where they could have been planted but, by a process of elimination, we think they must have been destined for Frog Hollow, which was located well beyond any tourist trail. It's so far from old tourist routes that no one would have seen if there were 'foreign' plants or not here. Otherwise, as mentioned previously, Belvoir's garden would surely never have been recognised as being one of the best gardens north of London, specifically famed for its limited use of exotic, imported plants.

The fishponds were built in 1802 and a year later the water from them was used to supply the newly built hunt kennels, a mile away, in the middle of the park. After 1803, records are rather vague. There is a dearth of information until 1909 when we have definite accounts and photographs of Frog Hollow being a bog garden. W H Divers writes about: 'A nice water garden Frog Hollow with rustic bridges and winding paths is halfway round [the Duke's Walk], and many varieties of conifers are growing near to it.'

OPPOSITE
THE NEWLY DREDGED LAKE
and recently installed pavilion

LEFT
DETAIL OF BROWN'S PLAN
showing the site of Frog Hollow

Diana Cooper described it, in 1918, as: 'Exactly like a transformation scene at Drury Lane, azaleas and syringa and asphyxiating smells...'[40]

The whole of Frog Hollow became part of our restoration programme by accident. Riding through it one Sunday morning with the children on their ponies, I noticed the lake was flooding – the overflow had disappeared and the Boat House was nearly submerged. Aunt Ursie recounted how it used to look in the 1920s, and I could see the bones of the design she described through the flooding and mass of trees, shrubs and weeds. It took three months with a digger to dredge the waterways and strip everything back. Apart from a disaster with a patch of Japanese knotweed, which was unwittingly dug up in one place and dumped in another and needed sterilising, it was all relatively easy to establish.

OPPOSITE
FROG HOLLOW, March 2015

ABOVE
9th DUKE OF RUTLAND, 31st March 1929, accompanied by his labrador, Bever, and his beloved bulldog, 'Johnny Bull' on the lake at Frog Hollow

[40] Lady Diana Cooper, *op. cit.*

OPPOSITE
EMMA WITH PHIL BURTT
at Frog Hollow, June 2015

BELOW
MALLARD is the staple duck for the shoots at Frog Hollow;
WICKER HORSE
by sculptor Laury Dizengremel stands in front of Frog Hollow's mallards, June 2014

RIGHT
MONTY, a yellow labrador

Phil Burtt has been particularly instrumental in the development of this garden because there were lots of pheasant rearing pens up on the hill and, without his expert guidance, the garden elements could have had a detrimental effect on the shoot. But he was sympathetic to the garden as well as to the shoot and carefully pushed back the pens from view; no one now would be any the wiser that the two elements work hand-in-glove.

During the shooting season, the water features have provided a natural duck shoot, which has proved very successful and a favourite with Guns. Brown gave very little advice on paper for Frog Hollow. Spyers' 1779 survey shows a stream – a feeder for the River Devon – springs and woodland, but it would have been an ideal spot to build a large pond for a duck decoy. These were particularly popular in the 17th century, and again 200 years later, for enticing wild ducks with decoys onto the water and under nets before capture. They became less relevant when shooting became popular in the mid-18th century, but for lead-shot-free duck meat for the table, they were essential. Brown would have seen many similar ponds in the wildfowl-rich Lincolnshire fenland as he journeyed in the area, and they frequently featured in his parks including Lowther, Packington and Croome. It doesn't seem at all sporting, but it may have saved many teeth.

It reminds me of the story about the Dowager Duchess Mary Isabella, widow of the 4th Duke. Legend has it that about the time she acquired the nickname 'Was-a-bella' for losing her youthful good looks, she lost a front tooth. Rather than live with an unsightly gap, a woman from the Estate was persuaded to part with one of her own as a substitute.

The position of the ponds, trees and natural planting set into the gentle hillside in this garden has a dreamy quality to it, which is very Picturesque in style. This corner of Brown's plan felt like a blank canvas for us to develop because it was so overgrown and bore no resemblance to his ideas for it. We had an opportunity to do something that really worked for us, as well as have some fun with the topography and the water. I like to think that Elizabeth must have felt the same when she added Picturesque touches to Brown's ideas, as she did in so many of the gardens here at Belvoir.

Very little new planting was needed, but we introduced five large magnolias 30 feet below the tree line to show off their flowers against the green background; gunnera and dogwoods have been placed in damp soil between the lakes to add colour and texture. A spring in the hillside inspired a 'Garden of Peace'. I had seen a stone ring at Chelsea Flower Show one year and thought how lovely it would be to try to recreate something similar here with the hill and trees behind it as a perfect backdrop.

Aunt Ursie came for a summer family barbecue when we had finished the project and she shrieked with excitement; it was just as she had remembered it from her own childhood. Our boys and their friends were playing in canoes on one pond and fishing for trout in another, while we grown-ups enjoyed the tranquility of the setting over a civilised picnic lunch. Aunt Ursie's approval means a lot and, together with our own pleasure in the results, it's the garden that we have had the most fun creating.

OPPOSITE
EMMA WITH PHIL BURTT, **admiring developments in Frog Hollow, June 2015**

RIGHT
FROG HOLLOW features a number of ornamental sculptures, including a stone ring

FROG HOLLOW
viewed from BLackberry Hill, May 2015. WILLOW HORSE SCULPTURE on the bank by Laury Dizengremel

CHAPTER NINE

THE PARKLAND

KNIPTON PASTURE

From frogs we metaphorically jump to a bull and leave the Duke's Walk at Frog Hollow to head east towards Granby Wood and King's Wood. These woods date back to 1817 and 1779 respectively, and the latter is shown on Spyers' survey as a genuine mediaeval park. By 1793, 290 trees had been felled from King's Wood and I'm assuming this could well have been another part of Joseph Hill's initiative to rescue the Estate's finances during the near-calamitous tenure of the 4th Duke and subsequent minority. But all these trees make up part of Brown's perimeter tree belt and are rich with mid-19th century oak and sweet chestnut, with older oak, beech and sycamore.

Brown had planned many of his rides and walks, which are so characteristic of his style, through these woods and we have been busy opening many of them up again for the tercentenary. Even with all the work we had done up to this point, my goosebumps raised when we heard the digger man had found something of interest. Out of dense overgrowth that appeared to have no practical, never mind aesthetic, purpose the men had found a raised walk that had been completely obliterated from view. It was obviously built for a reason, but it was only when we scrambled through it that we found the most beautiful private and idyllic spot. There are various small ponds, which have sadly silted up, but you can imagine carriages stopping to let out passengers for a stroll to an utterly glorious picnic site.

It can get a bit addictive to keep clearing the mess for the Brownian ideal and we were about to stop in this area, but we still wanted to open up the view from Knipton Pasture into Frog Hollow to keep it faithful to Brown's plan. Like every other clearing project, we discovered another story. As the digger moved deeper into the undergrowth we came across an old brick building that measured approximately 12 ft^2. John Phibbs was thrilled as he explained that it would have been the bull hovel, better known today as the bull shed. Brown often positioned these sheds in clear view for everyone to see the farm's prize bull from the driveway and Elizabeth must have been inspired to do the same.

THE CASTLE FROM HARSTON HILL over Briery Wood, June 2014

ABOVE
ELIZABETH, DUCHESS OF RUTLAND after 1824, George Sanders

Sometime after the Duchess's death the painter returned to Belvoir to add the Castle, Lakes and bridge

RIGHT
EMMA, May 2015

THE CHASE

Knipton is an important part of Belvoir's mediaeval history and it was of particular interest to Brown. It could well be that his idea to reinstate the chase originated from family stories about Knipton. The 5th Earl of Rutland (1576-1612) had bought a Manor of Knipton in the late 16th century, which included the Hall (later known as the Priory because it had gothic windows, not because of any ecclesiastical association) and the small 'Knipton Park' (later known as King's Wood). These were all good names to add weight to mediaevalist mythologies. Added to which there was a chase at Knipton, according to a Court of Survey in the 17th century, but it belonged to the Duchy of Lancaster – in a separate manor – and leased to the Dukes of Rutland. By the 18th century, it was held under the Crown by the Dukes of Newcastle and it wasn't until 1803 that the Enclosure Award of Knipton stated that the Duke of Rutland was Lord of the Manor. But, by then, there was no reference to the chase. Thus, the seeds of a chase had germinated from a grain of truth and grown into the perfect embodiment of Gothic taste, reflecting the cultural shifts of a changing political society.

The enchanting parkland views from this corner of Knipton are special for me. They bring back fond memories of early-married life when we lived at Knipton Lodge with four of our children. Hugo, the youngest, was born at the Castle. In Elizabeth's time, the trees would have been in their infancy, although large enough to give an impression of their appearance at maturity.

Leaving the woodland track in King's Wood brings us into Knipton Pasture. The drive from Knipton was already here when Spyers and Brown surveyed the Estate. The Marquis of Granby (heir to the 3rd Duke and who died before inheriting the Dukedom) wanted it to be much as it is today – a single grass plain. Letters in the Belvoir Archives between 1766 and 1767 show how involved Lord Granby was with planting. Huge amounts of 'seeds were shipped on board his Majesty's Ship Mermaid under Capt Dean's Care and to be delivered to the Ordnance Storekeeper at Plymouth or Portsmouth and by him to be forwarded to his Excellency the Marquis of Granby commander in Chief of his Majesty's forces &c &c &c'.[41]

ABOVE
ROGER MANNERS, 5TH EARL OF RUTLAND (1576-1612) Jeremiah van der Eyden

OPPOSITE
VIEW OF BELVOIR CASTLE FROM THE SOUTHWEST WITH BELVOIR HUNT IN FULL CRY, 1730, Thomas Badeslade

41. Belvoir Archives

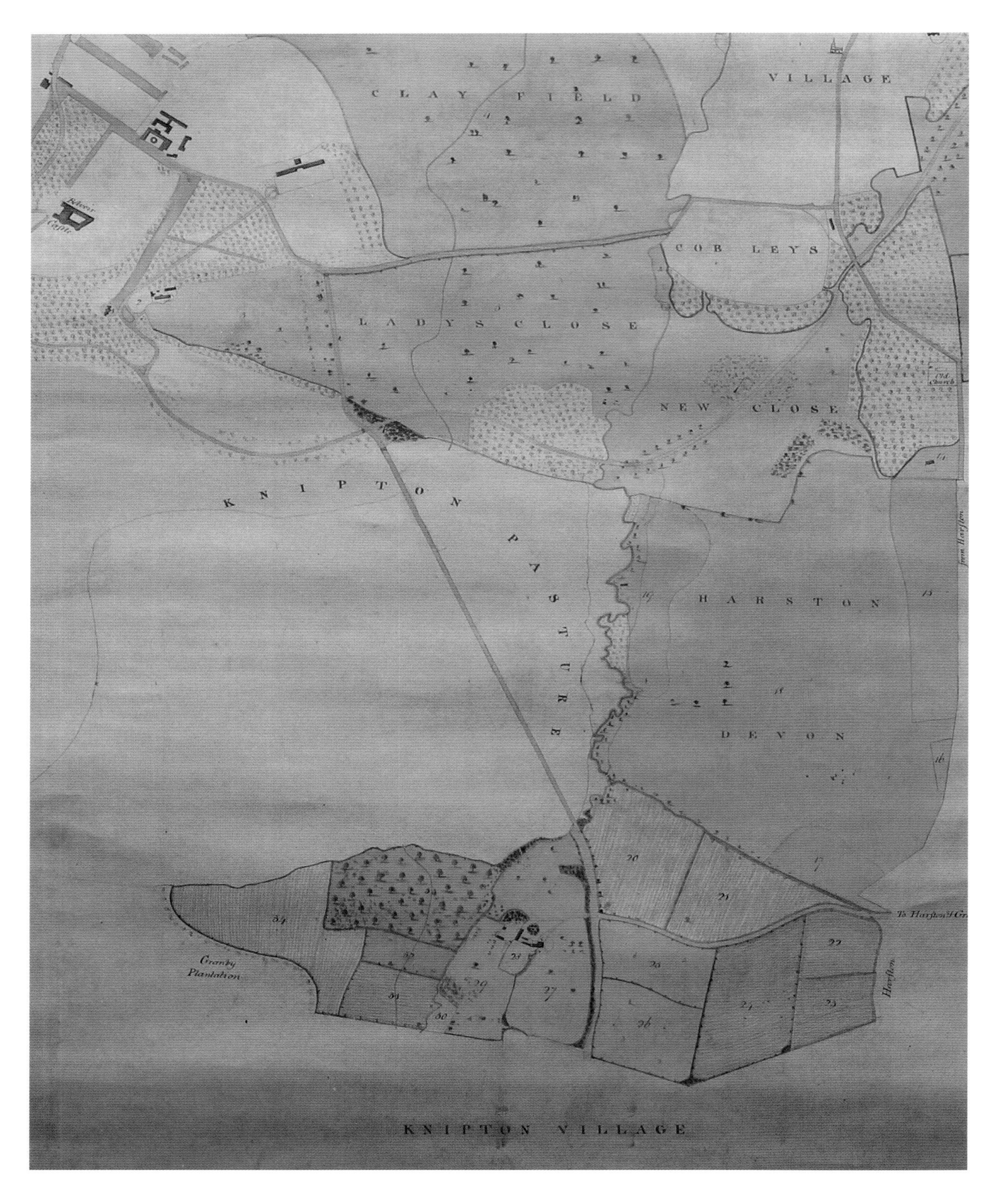

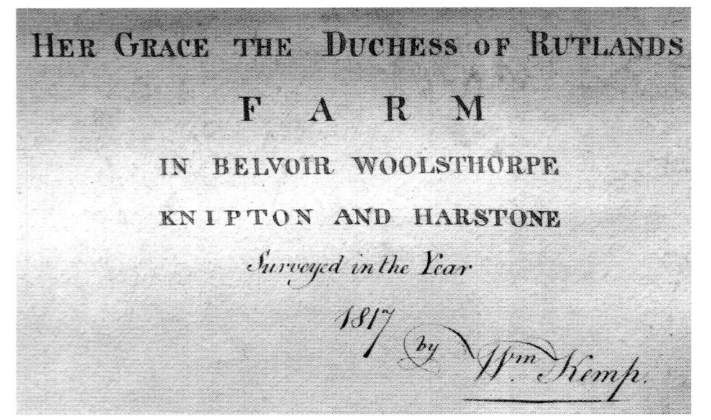

DEVON PARK

Looking across the Upper Lake to the east of the gatehouse is the cricket pitch. Back in 1817, it was marked on plans as a couple of arable fields on the Duchess's Model Farm. (The Model Farm was a working farm that was integrated into parkland. It was another element of the pastoral fantasy in a grand landscape garden.) Sadly, we were forced to cut down some very old trees – some dead and others dangerously close – on the edge of the pitch. Two of the trees marked for felling, an oak and a sweet chestnut, posed a mystery. The size of the girths suggested that they were over 300 years old and must have been planted in the early 18th century. But, on the 1817 map their position was not on a field boundary as we might have expected, but in the middle of a large arable field. Brown had a renowned reputation for his ability to move mature trees and there are possible examples near the Dairy. If he could move trees that were 100 years old then it is likely that these two trees, at least, were transplanted from somewhere else, too.

The cricket club has been an essential part of the local community since the Estate built the pavilion in 1932. More recently it has been home to the Belvoir Castle Cricket Trust – a registered charity focused on encouraging up to 2,000 children and young people per year to play cricket and engage in the countryside. We have been extremely fortunate to have some wonderfully generous support from many individuals and organisations including the MCC who have an annual match versus my team every summer. We've had some great days with all sorts of guests playing for both teams; Sir Tim Rice, Mike Gatting, Liam Botham, Anton Du Beke (star of *Strictly Come Dancing*) and many other well known faces. As well as cricket for local children, we organise supervised excursions on the Estate and discuss the land, farming, wildlife, the hunt, shoot and the amazing landscape that underpins the whole operation.

It's such a joy to see young faces genuinely absorbing our volunteers' enthusiasm for our country way of life.

This area was the cause of a dispute that went back to the 3rd Duke and Mr Welby who owned the Manor of Harston, in 1737. To stop Welby enclosing the village and parcelling land for himself, which the Duke wanted, the Belvoir Estate bought a farm at Harston. The resulting fall-out continued for over 50 years. With neither party budging, the dispute was still current for the 4th Duke, this time over enclosures and shooting rights. Joseph Hill advised the Duke to continue with the family's determination to have the land at Harston, especially the exclusive manorial and shooting rights or else Brown's woodland, which he proposed below the village of Harston and on top of Devon Park, would benefit Welby's pheasants. Such was the importance of Harston to Belvoir, that Hill even suggested throwing a sop into the pot: 'If Mr Welby will sell you the land you wish, I think your Grace would do well to offer him the Manor of Denton as a Present. Indeed the mere Feather cannot be estimated at much – I will observe besides that if Your Grace is too tenacious the Treaty will end without Effect – so I advise moderation.'[42] In a letter Hill wrote a month later, dated 17 November, 1786, he described how convinced he was that Mr Welby would not part with Harston and how they should battle it out. He wrote: 'The Inclosure of Harston is a great Object to Your Grace, as it enables you to make the Plantation Mr Browne recommended.'[43]

In the end, the matter was resolved and Harston was finally enclosed in 1788 but not until a year after the Duke had died. Perhaps it appealed to the 4th Duke and Brown's sense of humour to propose the main sweeping driveway right through the middle of the land in question. It really stuck two fingers up to the whole charade. What a shame neither Brown, the 3rd Duke, the Marquis of Granby or even the 4th Duke had the satisfaction of winning. Maybe the triumph had lost its potency by the time the 5th Duke and Duchess built the main drive further north through Brewer's Grave from the Denton Road. Or perhaps there was wit in its location: the Welby family, by now firmly ensconced in their new manor at Denton, would have surely seen Belvoir 'traffic' travelling along the newly planted avenue from their home to the ducal entrance on the edge of their estate. Happily, the Welby and Rutland families are excellent neighbours today and great family friends.

OPPOSITE
KEMP'S SURVEY for the Duchess's Model Farm, 1817

LEFT
DARREN BICKNELL AND ANTON DU BEKE at a celebrity cricket match in 2014

42. Belvoir Archives
43. Ibid.

Despite peace over Harston, Brown's woodland was never planted. Until now. It is another obvious place to honour Brown's tercentenary year by completing the missing section, which we did in the full glare of television cameras with Alan Titchmarsh in March, 2015. We have followed the sinuous shape of the outline from Brown's plan, although we have had comments from visitors about how the planting would not have been so grid-like in Brown's day. It's a valid point, of course, and one that our forestry manager is quick to justify by pointing out that in Brown's day there would have been armies of labourers to remove the weeds between the young trees. Nowadays, we have the advantage of machinery that cuts through the plantations in next-to-no-time, but you have to have enough space between the trees for the equipment to pass through.

As Joseph Hill said in 1787, in a couple of letters about securing land in Harston to the 4th Duke: 'The Allotment proposed for Your Grace at Harston is about 150 acres which is more than sufficient to effectuate Mr Brown's Plan...a great Part of the Beauty of Mr Brown's Plan will depend on the planting of Harston Hill.' Well it may well be over 200 years later, but we have at last effectuated this part of Mr Brown's plan and when it starts to mature it will undoubtedly add to its beauty. The same corner of land, which has been at the centre of so many rows over the centuries, has recently been at the heart of fresh conflict. And this time, it was our fault. When we planned our restoration projects we looked at the one-acre site of scrubby trees that were growing out of silted old ponds stepping up the hill towards Harston and thought it would be easy to chop them down, remove the silt and restore the ponds to their former glory. So we pulled out all the scrubby growth and started the dredging when, for various legal reasons, we had to stop.

In the end, it took two years to complete and there were times, given the area's history, when I thought this spot was jinxed. The ponds were originally dug out in 1826 after Elizabeth's death the previous year. The

Mill Pond and Upper Fish Pond are on contemporaneous plans and it's likely that Elizabeth's momentum to continue building on from the Lakes before she died was clung on to in the early stages of her family's collective grief. In her memory, and of those who were remembered by trees we have since felled at the end of the cricket field, we have renamed the ponds the Memorial Lakes. We have dug out 8,000 tons of silt and countless scrubby alder and willow trees that had self-seeded in ever-deepening silt over the last 30-40 years. To the untrained eye this healthy-looking alder carr looked like woodland, but it was murderous to the watercourse underneath and hazardously boggy underfoot. While the digger men were working they uncovered the early 19th-century culvert of the earlier ponds which was a nice, and reassuring, discovery. Now the Memorial Lakes are finished and stocked, they not only look amazing from many view points on the Estate, but their shape and position are definitely in keeping with Brown's style.

ABOVE
THE MISSING SECTION OF BROWN'S PERIMETER TREE BELT below Harston, has been planted with 5,200 native broadleaf trees

LEFT
THE MEMORIAL LAKES

THE LAKES

One of Brown's greatest engineering achievements in many of his landscapes was his breathtaking water features – dammed rivers became serpentine lakes or widened streams resembling rivers, all stretching into scenic backdrops and vistas. His design for Belvoir was river-like and, although it wasn't started until 1821 and its 10½-acre shape and position shifted slightly from the original, it is still a fine Brownian example of a body of water flowing through the valley floor with a bridge to conceal the change of level between two lakes. The greatest sadness is that although the Upper Lake was beginning to fill up before Elizabeth died in November 1825, she never saw the finished view.

LEFT
THE LOWER LAKE
as seen from the bridge

OPPOSITE
AN AERIAL VIEW of Upper and Lower Lakes to the left and Memorial Lakes to the right

Why construction of the Lakes began when it did is still a matter of conjecture. Information is sparse in the Belvoir Archives. The riverbanks in Lady's Close were being levelled and repaired in September 1820, which suggests that major investment to flood the area was not imminent. But, less than a year later, John Tyler & Co is mentioned in the Ledgers for building a dam. By the following summer, Knipton Mill, mapped on Spyers' survey on the River Devon, was dismantled and work started on the lower lake; 3,600 ft of earth were levelled, the waterfall was made, the culvert drains to the head were dug out, a 'Puddle Drain' was dug out and the bed was puddled with clay – the same process used to build canals. An entry in the accounts journal of '39 quarts of Ale @ 8d' suggests that the workmen were rewarded for their efforts.

Sixteen men from the Woods department, including other Estate workers drafted in from jobs on the plantations, roads and harvest worked on the construction of the Lakes over a three-year period. By the time of Elizabeth's death, the bridge was built and the Brewer's Grave drive was under construction, the riverbanks were built-up and levelled, and turfed to the water's edge. Of all the many practical purchases recorded to facilitate the building work, an entry for 'a Muscovy Duck and Drake' in August 1823, has the ring of a child's plea. At that time, Elizabeth's three youngest children, Charles, John and George were aged between eight and three, and I have a lovely mental picture of these little boys feeding tame ducks on their new lake.

It's nearly 100 years since these Lakes were dredged and there are plenty of family stories that have been passed down through the generations describing horses harnessed to chains and tools to drag silt out of the water. We have had quotes of up to £250,000 to dredge the Lakes today so we keep putting it off.

We have very little information about the design of the bridge. Whoever drew up the plans for this elegant, five-arched, ornamental feature, it is certainly Brownian in appearance. However, for such a tranquil spot, it seems particularly poignant that the bridge was also the site of a desperately sad family story – the tragic suicide in 1900 of 34-year-old Lady Kitty Manners, daughter of the 7th Duke of Rutland and his second wife, Janetta. Diana Cooper wrote about the event with characteristic spirit: 'Unarmed for life, artistic and frustrated, she sought and never found relief, neither by joining the Church of Rome nor by becoming a nurse at Guy's...These departures exasperated her eccentric mother (my grandfather's second wife), so Aunt Kitty, decked in what jewellery she possessed and marking the fatal brink with her parasol, found peace in the deep Belvoir lake.'[44] We have a heartbreaking letter in the archives from the 7th Duke to his son, Lord Granby, noting that he felt he

deserved the 'double chastisement' (having lost his second wife, Janetta, the year before). It seems he had been very worried about his daughter for some time and, judging by a letter of condolence to him from the Archdeacon, he had voiced concern several months before the fateful day. I have great sympathy for the 7th Duke who endured so much grief in his long life, starting at the age of seven when he lost his mother.

OPPOSITE (top)
JOHN MANNERS 7th DUKE OF RUTLAND (1818-1906), English School

OPPOSITE (below)
JANETTA, DUCHESS OF RUTLAND (1837-1899) 1891, English School

LEFT AND ABOVE
A TRADITIONAL 'BROWNIAN' five-arched bridge between Upper and Lower Lakes

[44] Lady Diana Cooper, *op. cit.*

Brown had planned various small clumps of trees either side of the Lakes but, on the whole, the land would have been open to maximise the views from the many vantage points in the parkland and from the Castle. Some of the oaks and turkey oaks are over 200 years old. It is probable that they were planted under the instruction of the Duke of Beaufort in the late 18th century. Austrian pines (*Pinus nigra)* on the east side match this date, too. Higher up the hill, between Old Church Plantation and Woolsthorpe village, are some of the oaks that were planted during the 4th Duke's tenure from acorns collected from Croxton Park.

TOP
HEREFORD CATTLE grazing on the banks of the Upper Lake

ABOVE
TRIANGULAR-SHAPED plantation of Austrian pines (*Pinus nigra*), seen from two directions

THE DEVON AND OLD CHURCH WOOD ABOVE BELVOIR UPPER LAKE viewed from the road to Woolsthorpe, spring 2015. On the slopes to the right of the Brownian stand of Austrian pine, a huge area of pasture has been planted with young trees, completing after a 230 year delay, Brown's parkland perimeter planting on Harston Hill. An ancient oak dating from before Brown's time, stands proudly in the foreground beyond an arable crop

THE KENNELS

The Manners family had been obsessed with hunting for generations. They had enjoyed the privileges of the mediaeval warren, the chase and two deer parks, and so it was probably no surprise that the prospect of fox-hunting, and the opportunity to jump all the new fences surrounding recently enclosed farms across the county, would be the next big craze for John of the Hill.

OPPOSITE
THE KENNELS FOR THE BELVOIR HOUNDS were built in the early 19th century to James Wyatt's designs

ABOVE
THE BELVOIR HOUNDS on their daily exercise today

LEFT
THE DUKE OF RUTLAND'S DOG PACK, Sir Francis Grant

The seminal moment may well have been recorded in Thomas Badeslade's painting *View of Belvoir Castle from the South West with Belvoir Hunt in Full Cry,* 1730. Although there is a record in the archives that talks of fox-hunting as early as 1540 at Croxton Park, it was probably a one-off. The Badeslade picture has often been assumed to represent stag-hunting but in *The History of the Belvoir Hunt 1899*, the author, T F Dale wrote: 'But a close examination of it shows that the hounds were steady from deer, and that the real object of their pursuit is a little red fox, which can be discerned making its way at best pace through the woods below the Castle.' The horses appear to be lean and quick and Dale couldn't help pointing out that the chaplain, pictured towards the rear, obviously couldn't keep up with the much faster and more exciting pace of fox-hunting, as he was mopping his brow. Whatever the quarry, the picture importantly illustrates a *par force* hunt and is described as a chase – so crucial to the expansion of Brown's mediaeval idea for his landscape design. It is more than possible that he would have seen the picture on his visit in 1780 and he would have been aware of the tradition.

ABOVE
VIEW OF BELVOIR CASTLE FROM THE SOUTHWEST WITH BELVOIR HUNT IN FULL CRY, 1730,
Thomas Badeslade

OPPOSITE
Hunt whippers-in with the Belvoir hounds

The 4th Duke was not as keen on hunting as his father and grandfather, but he was proud of the family pack. When he left for Dublin in 1784 as Lord Lieutenant of Ireland, Hill suggested lending the hounds, 'to some great Man, while your Grace is in Ireland, it would make a great Saving.' The Duke must have refused because a couple of weeks later Hill made another suggestion: 'If they are to be kept, I should think £1000 a year more than sufficient [that's roughly the equivalent of £130,000 today], in your Grace's absence, with proper management – but in this Point there has been & I am satisfied there always will be, a Fallacy, for great Part of the Produce of Croxton Park & the other Land in Hand goes to the Support of the Hounds...'

The cost of managing the deer was another expense but the hounds were saved. There were drainage costs at the time, too. Drying out the land would have had a significant impact on the ground for fox-hunting. Hare and stag-hunting followed a much steadier pace and horses would have fared much better in wet ground; foxes on the other hand were more agile and faster, and horses needed a surer foot.

The 5th Duke had inherited his passion for hunting from his grandfather and great-grandfather and, during the early years of his marriage, he seems to have been either in London attending his political and regimental public duties or at his hunting box (a property used specifically for hunting parties) in

RIGHT
THE MELTON HUNT BREAKFAST, Sir Francis Grant depicting key figures of the hunting fraternity who were all close friends of the 5th Duke

OPPOSITE
JOHN HENRY, 5th DUKE OF RUTLAND, George Sanders. He is seen wearing his robes for the coronation of George IV in 1820

OVER
THE BELVOIR HOUNDS leaving the kennels for their daily exercise

Wilsford in Lincolnshire. Elizabeth wrote to him a year after their wedding, in 1800: 'I do not envy the way in which you pass your mornings, I hope you are almost tired of living without me, I shall have no means of getting to Wilsford...but you must give up hunting on Tuesday or Wednesday and come over to see me else I shall say you like hunting better than me.'[45] It's easy to see why she was so occupied with the building of the Castle and the development of the gardens as her husband was distracted by hunting for much of his early married life. In a letter to her five years later, in August 1805, after a 'fatiguing days shooting' grouse on the family's grouse moor in Derbyshire, he offered her fabulously comforting reassurance that: 'I like an affectionate wife, more than hunting or shooting'.

These were the glory days for hunting in Leicestershire when Melton Mowbray was the epicentre of the Cottesmore, Quorn and Belvoir packs. The 5th Duke, who was active Master of Foxhounds from 1804-1830, welcomed every Tom, Dick and Dandy to the Castle. Beau Brummell, the Prince of Wales, the Duke of York, the Duke of Argyll, the Marquis of Lorne, Lord Alvanley and Lord Jersey were all frequent visitors.

[45] Belvoir Archives

ABOVE
HOUND EXERCISE, Sir Alfred Munnings

BELOW
HUNTING SCENE NEAR BELVOIR CASTLE, John Ferneley. The 5th Duke is seen on his grey horse in the distance with his brothers, Lieutenant General Lord Charles Manners, on the left, and Major General Lord Robert Manners in the foreground

In contrast to the sporting fields of the hunt, Brown loved his walks and he liked to create regular diversions and resting places along the way. Following on from this tradition, the 5th Duke and Duchess laid out Kennel Walk, which meanders through Briery Wood – formerly Gorsey Close, a well known fox cover – from the bottom of the Spring Gardens across Knipton drive and down to the kennels. The Ledgers curiously record: 'Kennel Walk' January 1814 and 10 men, 2 boys and 1 woman drink Marquis's health.' George, the young Marquis at that time, would have been five months old.

When the kennels were built in 1802, many outsiders questioned the decision to move them from Woolsthorpe and to stick them slap bang in the middle of the parkland. The writer John Claudius Loudon (a follower of Picturesque) made a dry comment in 1806: 'Every useful building is always an apology to the improver for finding a picturesque object or composition. Even DOG-KENNELS will effect this purpose. They should always be placed distant from the mansion, as well as excluded from the most exquisite passages of scenery. Those at Belvoir are excellent; but their situation will probably be regretted by some...'[46]

[46] John Claudius Loudon, *A treatise on Forming, Improving and Managing Country Residences*, 1806

PREVIOUS PAGE
YOUNG HOUND PUPPIES,
June 2015

RIGHT
THE OCTAGONAL ROOF
on the kennels was part of James Wyatt's design to absorb noise

OPPOSITE
The village of Woolsthorpe below Cliff Wood, which was planted shortly after Brown's death

Brown had made no provision for the kennels to be moved from Croxton, where the 3rd Duke and his son, the Marquis of Granby, had spent so many happy days hunting from Croxton Park. But James Wyatt, who was rebuilding Elizabeth's Valhalla with towers and turrets, was also tasked with creating the design. The 5th Duke made frequent observations of the progress which he shared with his wife in letters. The Picturesque style didn't shy from exposed utility areas if they were beautifully designed, and Wyatt's architecture is certainly attractive and the octagonal roof was specially designed to absorb noise from hound cry. It is clear that Brown took fox-hunting within the parkland seriously as he retained in his plan Gorsey Close (Briery Wood), opposite the Kennels, which was an important fox cover.

Hunting has always been a social occasion and not just for the mounted field but for spectators, too. The topography surrounding Belvoir is ideal for finding a spot on high ground for following hounds. Many of the best views can also be seen from the Castle windows but there are various prospect points in the parkland that appear to have been built for this purpose, namely the east and south sides of Blackberry Hill, the top of the Duchess's Garden, the west side of Windsor Hill and further out in Old Park Wood and Cliff Wood. It is possible that they were built during the Civil War as defensive positions, but the most logical explanation is that they were viewing platforms for spectators to follow hounds when they had run out of the views from the Castle windows and terraces. The one in Cliff Wood is linked to parkland at the old St. James's Church in Woolsthorpe by a riding that is Brownian in style, suggesting they could well have been built together in the 1780s.

Some of the oldest trees in the parkland are in Kennel Wood. There are some 500-year-old oak trees in good health, and one or two others that have suffered from serious wind or snow damage that to me are unsightly. Our forestry advisor, Richard Sochacki, is always keen to remind me that decaying trees, provided they aren't a public danger, are wonderful habitats for wildlife such as insects, beetles, bats, nesting birds, and fungi. Just opposite Kennel Wood, at the bottom of Briery Wood, is a Site of Special Scientific Interest (SSSI) and home to the largest heronry in Leicestershire.

We planted some new cedar trees at the bottom of Briery Hill a few years ago but they failed. The ground turned out to be wetter than we realised but we persevered with different species, and western red cedars (*Thuja plicata*) are doing well in the damper conditions.

Cedars continue over the crossroads towards the Brewer's Grave drive with a beautiful double avenue of roughly alternating cedar of Lebanon and Himalayan cedars (*Cedrus deodara)*, with an outer avenue of Corsican pine (*Pinus nigra*). The Douglas fir (*Pseudotsuga menziesii*) appear to be over 200 years old and could well be the ones referred to in the Ledgers that were being fenced in the spring of 1821. They line the drive, towards the Lakes and the very old plantation of yew trees before the bridge, some more than 500 years old.

OPPOSITE
UPTURNED STUMPS: The Estate is managed to UK Woodland Assurance Standards which maintain bio-diversity and part of that is retaining 20 m^3 of standing and fallen dead wood per hectare

GREY HERON (*Ardea cinera*). From MacGillivray's watercolour drawings of British Animals (1831-1841), Natural History Museum, London
Ardea cinerea / Natural History Museum, London, UK / Bridgeman Images

ABOVE
CEDAR OF LEBANON (*Cedrus libani*) on the double avenue with Himalyan cedar (*Cedrus deodara*) and Douglas fir (*Pseudotsuga menziesii*)

PREVIOUS PAGE
AERIAL VIEW OF WOOLSTHORPE PARK
with the driveway from Brewer's Grave crossing over the bridge with the hunt kennels on the left

RIGHT
THE OLD ST. JAMES'S CHURCH
at Woolsthorpe. Watercolour by the 5th Duke's Agent, William King, *c.* 1799, before Elizabeth rebuilt the Castle and demolished the ruined church. The third Castle is on the left

OPPOSITE
SPYERS' SURVEY
clearly showing the avenue through Bushy Lady's Close later known as Ladies Close Plantation

WOOLSTHORPE PARK

From the bridge looking east through a gully filled with rhododendrons and silver birch is the site of the former St. James's Church – the focal point that never really was. Partly destroyed in 1643 by Parliamentary forces during the Civil War, Brown intended its ruined remains to stand as a Gothic monument to the family's history and a focal point at the end of a ride that cut through Lady's Close Plantation and Kennel Wood. Elizabeth, however, dismantled it; all that remains now is a grassed over mound of rubble. Instead of a Gothic ruin to catch the eye, she planted a garden. The Ledgers record John Smart, Ed and John Poizer and Ed Mears, 'Pruning trees and making a small garden by the Church at Woolsthorpe' in April-June, 1822.

Spyers mapped an avenue, formed by the break in the plantation, which would have framed both the view of the river from the church, and one of the church from the Castle. Brown must have been happy with the status quo because not only did he leave it unaltered on his plan, he also lined it up with a monument on Blackberry Hill. And yet for all the great ideas, the view was filled in during the 5th Duke's minority on the orders of the Duke of Beaufort. Joseph Hill had pleaded with the 4th Duke to allow the part-time agent at Belvoir, Mr Fillingham (he was also the agent at the Duke of Newcastle's Newark Estate) to grow their own trees because the cost of buying them in was too expensive: 'I wish your Grace would put the Leicestershire Planting under the Care of Mr Fillingham. He seems to think there has been a good deal of expense in buying of Plants at high Prices – of which indeed I heard before – but he advises a Nursery – of 5 or 6 acres – which is what I have long recommended – & is absolutely necessary if your Grace means to continue your Planting yearly...'[47] The correspondence illustrates how the finer points of landscape design could easily have been overlooked in the absence of a permanent and dedicated resident. Although the 4th Duke left for Dublin in 1784 and never returned, his staff fed him a stream of news. For example, Mr Fillingham wrote on 25th June, 1787: 'I flatter my self Your Grace will approve of the Plantations already done... Woolsthorpe old Church Plantation which we did last Winter will be a fine Ornament one day or other to Your Graces Castle...'[48]

The Old Church Plantation formed part of Brown's perimeter tree belt, and was to link up to the narrow belt of trees to the south of Woolsthorpe village at Cob Leas. But planting was abandoned when the Brewer's Grave Approach was built in 1808; all that remains now is a walk or 'riding' in Brown parlance.

47. Belvoir Archives
48. Ibid.

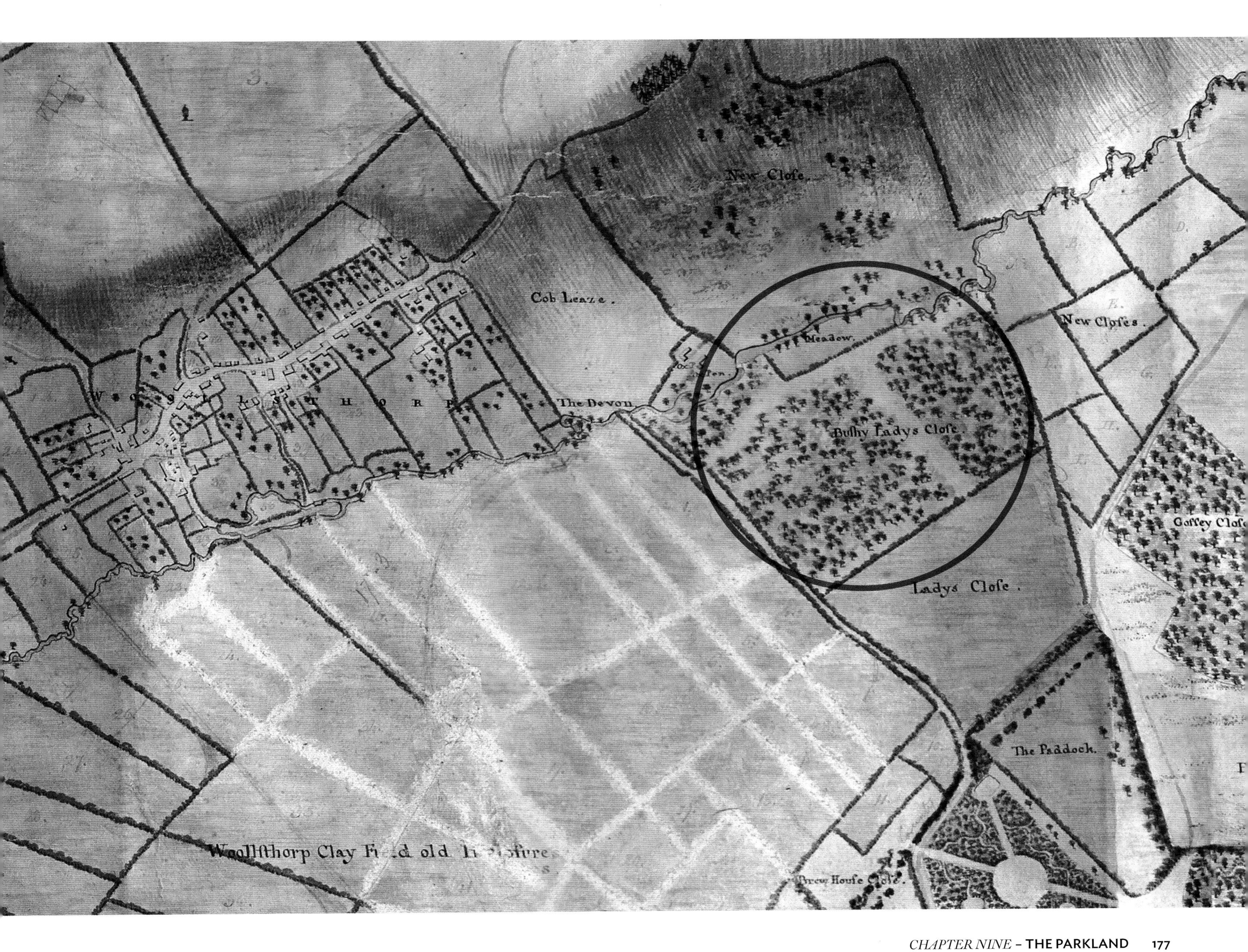
New Cloſe.
Cob Leaze.
The Devon
Meadow.
Buſhy Ladys Cloſe.
New Cloſes.
Ladys Cloſe.
The Paddock.
Brew Houſe Cloſe.

There were small-scale sand quarrying exploits in the 18th century and Spyers marked them on his survey. Areas of ridge and furrow, remnants from the open field systems for Woolsthorpe, are just about recognisable and there is an interesting bank at the junction with Devon Park with mature trees growing on it that has marked the parish boundary for hundreds of years.

The slope down to the river is visible from the Castle and was a favourite spot of Elizabeth's and, subsequently, Janetta. Janetta and the 7th Duke endured unbearably heavy loss as many of their children succumbed to tragic deaths.

As well as the desperately unfortunate Lady Kitty drowning in the lake, another child had died in infancy, another of tuberculosis aged 39, one in the First World War aged 45, and two more in their 20s of unknown causes. Their parents' agony must have had little respite. Brown had planned several clumps of trees for here. It is difficult to tell if they were ever planted but we are going to plant them in 2016, both in his memory and that of the 7th Duke's family.

OPPOSITE
HEREFORD CATTLE on Lady's Close opposite the Brewer's Grave Approach

ABOVE (left)
OLD CHURCH PLANTATION originally planted with oak, lime, beech, cherry, sycamore, wild cherry, Corsican pine and European larch, has been thinned and mostly replanted with oaks

ABOVE (right)
'ELIZABETH'S' CASTLE with the 'new' St. James's Church, Woolsthorpe

OVER PAGE
THE BREWER'S GRAVE APPROACH seen from the Castle

BREWER'S GRAVE APPROACH

This area, strictly speaking, is outside Brown's perimeter tree belt that we have used to define his parkland landscape but, because it later became the chosen site for the main drive and because he had proposed some planting here, we have included it. Perhaps the rumpus between the 4th Duke and Mr Welby over the Harston Enclosure had put everyone off building Brown's sweeping entrance from there, or maybe it was an easy option because the route had been used as a temporary drive in the 1790s while the Woolsthorpe Drive was planned and built. Either way, the 5th Duke and Duchess positioned their main drive from the Denton Road and, in 1807, the Brewer's Grave Approach was completed.

Woolsthorpe was enclosed in 1734 and, during the late 1700s, this area was transformed into a small quarrying site in an effort to source stone for road-building. (Quarrying resumed again between 1883-1921.) The results of this have left a fascinating, pockmarked landscape scarred with scoops, hollows and raised earthworks. Other weird anomalies in the levels are the part-remains of ridge and furrow, abandoned lanes and paths and the probable dumping of spoil by labourers working on the new Denton to Woolsthorpe public road that was finally completed in 1801, 20 years after it began.

From 1785, Hill and Fillingham were doing everything they could to improve access on the Estate, and planting nurseries, but all with very limited cash. Road materials had to be sourced on site to save money and workmen alternated between planting and road-building according to the weather and time of year. Fillingham had made a plan for the 4th Duke in November 1785, but stressed: 'I think it nearly impossible to make Roads with the Materials in the Neighbourhood that will remain fit for coaches or Chaise to pass where Waggons and Carts come.' His answer was to make private drives on grass, through the enclosures for family use in dry months only, to keep costs down.

OPPOSITE (left)
KAKOO, WIFE OF THE 9th DUKE on the driveway to Brewer's Grave, 1928

OPPOSITE (right)
THE GATES were brought from the family's other home at Cheveley Park, near Newmarket, after it was sold by the 7th Duke in 1893

LEFT
THE DIP IN THE GROUND marks the site of an old mediaeval track

This was actually an idea that Brown frequently used, but Hill did not agree with it. As Fillingham highlights in a letter to the Duke, on Christmas Day, 1785: 'Mr Hill says he don't approve of private Roads, Yet in my Opinion they will answer the best in every particular (except that of having a few more gates to open)...'

Sourcing gravel remained an issue for many years and the 5th Duke wrote to Elizabeth, in 1807, about using gravel from a relative's estate in Nottinghamshire for a walk in the Pleasure Grounds, stressing: 'But it is very scarce, and he says it may not be used in any other way, meaning on the roads'.

Brown had proposed three clumps of trees, one of which is Holywell Wood – a key component of the later driveway – one at Cliff Wood to the north and Young Oaks that join up to the Old Church Plantation. All three woods were planted soon after the 4th Duke's death in 1788. Holywell Wood is typically Brownian with a clump of oak in the centre of a ring of beech and horse-chestnut. There is no evidence to prove that the planting style is his but, interestingly, it is similar to a clump at Bowood, a landscape he laid-out in 1762. Another Brownian trademark in this wood is that the scarp appears to have been built up before planting – he used the technique to add drama to a composition or to hide

unwanted views; examples survive at Milton Abbey and Weston Park. In this case, it helped to obscure the village of Woolsthorpe from the east, if you were driving away, and the avenue from the Castle. With two other clumps on his plan visible to the north and south, all of which illustrate his methods for framing views, it seems possible that Brown could have verbally suggested to the 4th Duke running a drive from this approach, if the Harston Enclosure was lost. We'll never know.

The crowning glory of the whole hill is the beech avenue, not just for its visual magnificence now but for the skilled woodsmanship deployed in its planting. If you look carefully, you'll notice that the trees appear to be roughly three ages. The oldest are nearly 230 years old and would have been transplanted in 1808 as 30-year-old pollards from the 4th Duke's plantations. They stand comfortably next to slightly younger trees planted from nursery stock at the same time.

THE DOUBLE BEECH AVENUE
with trees dating back to the 1780s

Trees planted about 70 years ago as replacements are maturing nicely and then there are young trees we planted in 2007 to fill in gaps. There has been a suggestion to fell all the old trees and start again because it seems that just as the new trees become established, a branch from a neighbouring old tree invariably breaks off in a storm and either damages a young tree or smashes it completely. It's a costly problem as well as being disheartening, but it takes a lot of guts to fell one beautiful old tree never mind an entire avenue. So, for now we have compromised, and every new tree is planted in the original planting station. The old stumps are ground out very carefully and each new tree is fenced by an individual stockade to prevent terminal damage from livestock.

OPPOSITE
THE LODGE at Brewer's Grave

RIGHT
DELICATELY COLOURED PLANS and elevations by the Estate's own Architect, Mr Shelbourn, dated 1885:
(above) **the porch front;**
(below) **the porch side**

OPPOSITE
THE OCTAGONAL-ROOFED DAIRY was designed by James Wyatt and built in 1813

RIGHT (above)
THE DAIRY in 1890
Mary Evans Picture Library / Francis Frith

RIGHT (below)
THE DAIRY viewed from the Japanese Woodland

THE DAIRY

The Dairy, built for Elizabeth in 1813 from a plan by James Wyatt, was a working dairy and part of the Duchess's Model Farm, and she took the running of it very seriously. At the time, it was fashionable to practice mixed agricultural experiments on landed estates. The Earl of Leicester at Holkham and the Duke of Bedford at Woburn were pioneering developments on model farms on their own estates. Brown was a great advocate of farming too, and he liked to position model farms within the controlled setting of his parkland. He described his work at Croome, Trentham and Adderbury in Oxfordshire as farms.

Contiguous land at Belvoir had already been drained in 1804. The 5th Duke wrote to Elizabeth, in May of that year, and explained that: 'The closes next to Ladies Close are come into my hands and by taking the fence that separates them away they will make an excellent milking pasture for the cows. The old pasture that is so boggy, is according to your request about to be drained...' We found a fascinating newspaper clipping in Elizabeth's sketchbook that describes how hands-on she was, literally: 'The Dss of R...like a Noble "Shepherdess", an Honour to England, delights in feeding, with her own hands, the lamb that peacefully thrives under her auspices, and frisks on the meadows of Belvoir Castle.' Her stock included buffalo, Yorkshire bulls, Alderneys and Scotch Oxen, plus the tenants' cattle by 'Agistment'.

Wyatt's Gothic Dairy at Belvoir was designed as a working dairy and, in 1821, Elizabeth wrote to tell her husband that she was looking for a new 'Queen of the Dairy'[50] because the present one had to leave and get married. Elizabeth liked to walk there and check on progress. It wasn't unusual for her to set up picnics outside in the garden that she had planted.

The Dairy has always been painted pink and, framed by very beautiful 18th and 19th century oaks and sweet chestnuts overlooking an ancient triangular shaped paddock, it has a sort of surreal gingerbread-house quality to it.

[50] Belvoir Archives

The mature trees at the east end of the paddock, along the private driveway between Knipton and Belvoir, have an interesting history that if true, is also a bit surreal. Spyers drew a straight row of trees, next to a wall (now gone), on his 1779 survey. There aren't any trees in a straight line any more, only a group of oaks that date to the mid-18th-century and grow in an irregular line, as if they have been 'shuffled'. John Phibbs thinks this could be an example of one Brown's typical methods of 'softening' landscape architecture. Brown was well known for moving well-established trees if he thought they were in the wrong place and may well have suggested moving these trees to the 4th Duke, or one of his agents.

OPPOSITE
DAIRY AVENUE in Elizabeth's time was grass and she walked most days to check on work at the Dairy, then continued along the avenue to the walled kitchen garden (bottom)

BELOW
THE PADDOCK in front of the Dairy was marked on Spyers' survey and has remained unchanged

WOOLSTHORPE AVENUE

Brown had big ideas for this part of the parkland, proposing an elaborate and complex design consisting of a private drive flanked with a double avenue and two ridings: one grass and one gravelled within the tree belt, and a new public road on the northern edge. His best examples of long approaches include the Chesterfield Approach at Chatsworth, the London Approach at Petworth and the six-mile avenue from Blandford at Milton Abbey. His Woolsthorpe avenue would have been considered quite modest by comparison.

The Estate's workmen were building public roads in the late 18th century and this one was viable by 1792. It's likely that costs and trouble sourcing materials negated Brown's plans to indulge in the private drive and it was never built, nor was the planting implemented. It wasn't until the Queen's Silver Jubilee, in 1977, when the villagers planted the small-leaved lime (*Tilia cordata*) avenue from Woolsthorpe to halfway towards the Castle, that Brown's avenue first featured on the landscape. By coincidence, the Estate completed it in 2012, which happened to be the year of the Queen's Diamond Jubilee.

The heavy clay in this part of the park can be ruinous in wet weather for park events. Our first independent game fair in 2004 finished up in a quagmire from particularly heavy rain and, in the last week leading up to the CLA Game Fair in 2012, we watched helplessly as 13 inches of rain fell in three days. It was impossible to finish building the stands, never mind allow for traffic. The mud was catastrophic and it was a huge blow to everyone when the decision was made to cancel the whole event.

ABOVE AND OPPOSITE
THE SMALL-LEAVED LIME AVENUE along the public road from Belvoir to Woolsthorpe. Brown proposed the avenue in a far more elaborate scheme. It remained unplanted until 1977 and was finished in 2012

As the avenue turns to the southwest, with the Castle entrance on one side and Belvoir Lodge (the Old Peacock Inn) and the Elizabethan Court House on the other, you can see Saltbeck Plantation in the distance. By 1883, the Ordnance Survey showed all this area to the north of the Castle as parkland. Elizabeth had a walk built there in the autumn of 1819 and she designed a garden with roses around a spring.

A big project during our restoration programme was to clear out the scrubby hawthorn, blackthorn and elder overgrowth and dead elms from the Engine Yard (another functional Picturesque building, like the Kennels and the Dairy) on the Redmile and Woolsthorpe crossroads. It has let in so much light to this corner and exposed the buildings that in their day would have been full of joiners, plumbers and other tradesmen's workshops, as well as a forge for the blacksmith. It is now enclosed with a new post and rail fence in the Belvoir style and a young holly hedge.

As one lot of fencing goes in, another seems to come out. Along from the visitors' car park is a grassy bank that we have opened up by removing an old fence that was serving no purpose. The site has been attracting picnickers for generations. Before the 6th Duke succeeded to the Dukedom in 1857, he was often seen befriending the local gypsies who used to set up camp under the trees on this spot. He was quite an accomplished artist and he painted a rather beautiful picture of a red-cloaked Beatta Smith, the handsome daughter of the local gypsy king, Absalom Smith. I'm sure tongues would have wagged, as the handsome Lord Granby's friendship would no doubt have been considered by many to be inappropriate. There is a letter in the archives from a Miss Gooding to Lord Granby's brother, Lord John (later 7th Duke) that makes a reference to: 'Granby's Fair – or rather Brown friends'.

RIGHT
BELVOIR LODGE
formerly the Old Peacock Inn

OPPOSITE
NORTH ELEVATION of the Castle from meadows towards Woolsthorpe

OLD PARK

Spyers mapped the whole area, from Saltbecks and the Engine Yard to Church Thorns, as Old Park – it had been a properly licensed park from 1304-1460, and it must have excited Brown, given his intention to create much of the whole landscape in mediaeval style. But he made it clear that this area was not to be a deer park. He wanted it for a mowing lawn of about 300 acres surrounded by a belted ride; it would have provided hay and fresh grass to feed the Duke's horses. Meadows would be mown on alternate years and grazed by horses or deer in between times. As he wrote in his plans: 'The Lawn with Plantations round it, to be Mowed and Fed occasionally' and as 'Intended Lawn to be Occasionally divided for Hay &c.'

The writer John Parnell noted, in 1769, a similar feature at Hagley Hall in Warwickshire: 'This Part of the Park is kept for hay every second year', and added: 'This is a piece of good management almost universally observed in the best Parks in England.'[51] From the Castle it would have provided a typically beautiful view, with or without grazing animals.

Brown proposed to strip out the boundary hedge between Calcraft Close and Windmill Close, and flesh out the trees in the hedging into clumps. Old Park was fenced in 1809, and again in 1818 and the old boundary is clearly visible along the public footpath. The tree clumps, for all their Brownian appearance, have been replanted – today's trees are all less than 50 years old.

Spyers' survey finished at Church Thorns, although Brown continued his plans into the warren with rides all the way to Stathern Point. It wasn't unusual for him to go beyond a survey; he had done something similar when he worked at Bowood, amongst other plans. And, it wasn't unusual to plant warrens with evergreens. He had done just the same at Ampthill in Bedfordshire in 1770.

The Duke of Beaufort and Joseph Hill began the afforestation of the warren during the 5th Duke's minority. Nichols described the progress as: 'Plantations...now making on all the neighbouring hills; Stathern point, now planting, and the whole country...improving so fast in the beauty and profit, under the auspices of his grace of Beaufort...'[52]

A lot of timber was sold in these woods in 1787 to restore the family's finances. One batch from Barkstone Wood fetched £3,400 (£440,000 in today's money). It's a business model that we have used during our own restoration programme. We have thinned the woods by taking out European larch,

BELOW
HARE & RABBIT,
Watercolours by Nick Hugh McCann

OPPOSITE
A VERY BROWNIAN VIEW
of the Castle as seen from the old 'Warrener's Cottage' now called the Woodlands Cottage, and a drawing by Col Frederick Trench in 1819 from a very similar position

[51] John Parnell, *Journal of a Tour thro' England and Wales*, 1769. The parkland accounts of Felbrigg in Norfolk also point to biennial harvesting
[52] J. Nichols, *op. cit.*

oak, ash and sycamore. The larch is prone to a new disease called *Phytophthora ramorum*, which can also kill oak, so we have removed as much of it as we can. Other trees prone to new diseases are ash from ash-dieback and oaks from acute oak decline. Early external symptoms of the latter disease are shown in dark weeping patches on tree stems which can result in severe crown deterioration. So far the condition is known to occur only in England and, worryingly, particularly in the Midlands. The proceeds from much of the timber sales have gone straight back into replanting and restoration of the landscape.

Hill advocated planting many additional plantations on the Estate: 'That would not only add great Beauty to it, when they are grown, but will afford Protection & Warmth to some bleak Parts of it, particularly on the Summit of Branston & Eaton Hill...& a small Spot over Barkston Wood – Here I should prefer Firs – or mixed, at least, with Oaks. There is a great want of Timber likewise on the Farms both for Ornament & use...'[53]

Before we leave Old Park, it's impossible not to be struck by the view of the Castle from here. We've already discussed how important the reverse view is to the Castle, but this angle is absolutely timeless. The viewing platform, raised on a mound is clearly identifiable. John Phibbs tells me Brown's plans would have used this area to create a rather theatrical entrance from Stathern Point. You can imagine the old Warrener's Cottage, screened by trees, with an 'azure curl of smoke... beneath the sheltering coppice.' There would have been a similar scene outside a second cottage, which existed further eastwards, with the Castle as the third point to make a classic Picturesque composition. There is a sense of being lured into the view as the topography almost funnels you towards Belvoir, past a scene of bucolic bliss.

Our journey cuts along a track from an Estate cottage into Brown's proposed wood that became known as Sir John's Belt – a spot where today's keepers regularly have to move on drivers and their companions caught behind steamy windows. It ends at the crossroads opposite the Sawmill where we take the public road on the route of the private carriageway to Croxton Park, back towards the Castle.

The glimpses through the roadside trees down to the ponds in Frog Hollow and the rhododendrons in late spring are spellbinding. The road roughly follows the line of the hill's

apex to the south and High Leys to the north, where a couple of monkey puzzle trees grow and a single wellingtonia (*Sequoia dendron giganteum*). Evergreens continue beyond the public roads onto the private carriage drive to Croxton and are typical of Brown's planting plans to differentiate private drives from public roads. Thomas Whately wrote in 1770 about how to distinguish a riding or avenue from a public road: 'Plantations of firs, whether placed on the sides of the way, or in clumps or woods in the view'.[54] John Phibbs describes it as 'sleeve' planting; it suggests an informal avenue, but also controls the views from the road.

Leaving the road to the bottom of Blackberry Hill takes us through Sligo Gate. There is nearly always a story behind the names of drives on the shoot, woods and gardens, and Sligo Gate is named after the Earl of Sligo who, as family legend has it, accidentally 'pinked the Keeper's arse' during a shoot, in 1892. There was a fine for accidentally peppering a keeper or beater with gunshot and the Earl was obliged to pay him five shillings. The keeper survived the humiliating ordeal, but the poor chap's bottom would have been scarred for life.

OPPOSITE (left to right)
A WELLINGTONIA AND TWO MONKEY PUZZLE TREES dominate High Leys, and RIGHT
A MONKEY PUZZLE TREE stands sentinel opposite Sligo Gate

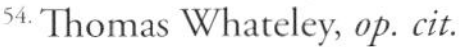

[53] Letter from Joseph Hill to the 4th Duke of Rutland, 10th April 1787
[54] Thomas Whateley, *op. cit.*

CHAPTER TEN

BLACKBERRY HILL

Evidence of human activity on this extraordinary flat, roughly triangular peak jutting above Castle Hill dates back to Roman times. The survival of Roman artefacts and its close proximity to the Roman road, which ran through the vale from Margidunum at Saxondale in Nottinghamshire to the Fosse at Six Hills in Leicestershire, suggests that this spot was likely to have been a defensive position. By 1067, when Robert de Todeni was awarded the Estate he chose the Castle Hill for his motte-and-bailey, presumably because the location, although a little lower, dominates a much wider region.

Battles aside, by the 17th century it had been planted with woodland. A series of radial rides ran through it and there was a large central etoile. The 1731 Badeslade drawings in *Vitruvius Britannicus* show Blackberry Hill looking extremely exposed, with a regimented avenue of trees and deer on the top. We can only assume that it must be the same avenue that features in Spyers' survey, as a circuitous route set within the perimeter. Brown planned to remove it and soften the table-top hill with clumps of different species. He rarely planted avenues within parkland but his proposals to remove this one may also have been part of his plan to reinstate the chase, which required wide-open spaces. He also made plenty of allowance for shooting with strategic planting that would force birds to fly over specific drives, and this is something that we continue to maintain for our own shoot today.

The only other feature that Brown wanted for Blackberry Hill, apart from trees, was an obelisk of some kind. It is marked on his plan in the middle of the hill in alignment with the ruined St. James's Church on the opposite side of the park, above the lakes. No monument was ever built and, even now as we've been considering how best to remember Brown's contributions to the landscape at Belvoir, an obelisk would not work here because it would tower into the middle of a very important pheasant drive.

OPPOSITE
BLACKBERRY HILL
with its curiously man-made looking appearance; the highest point on the Estate. Cover crops for the shoot dominate the planting. A new sweet chestnut avenue has been planted on the outer grass perimeter strip

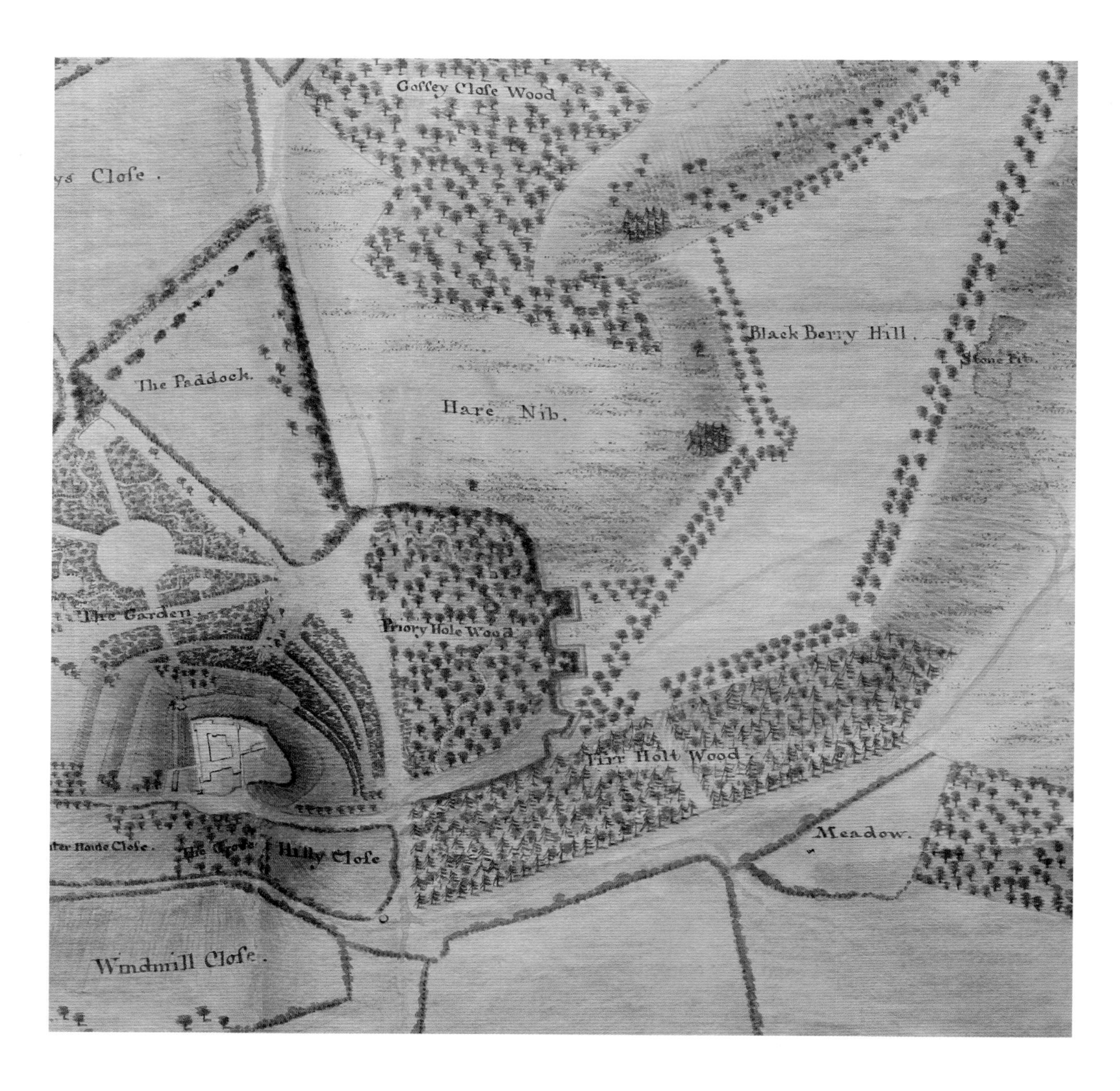

ABOVE
BLACKBERRY HILL
shown on Spyers' survey of 1779. Every cartographer of the region has included an avenue on the hill. It has been replanted twice since Brown reworked the avenue seen here

Elizabeth had her own plans for Blackberry Hill and reinstated the avenue in about 1804 with sweet chestnuts. She kept Brown's clumps of sycamore, lime, beech, oak, turkey oak and London plane. Records show that the agent, King was, 'taking up Trees at the Hills and planting them'. We can only assume that the trees were taken from one of the Estate's plantations like the one at Branstone Flatts, planted in 1788. Despite Elizabeth's reworking of Brown's plans here, her avenue is best described as a parade. There are old family stories of some of the work near Blackberry Hill being carried out by prisoners of war from a camp built at Norman Cross during the Napoleonic Wars. There is a model of a ship that is on display in the old kitchens that was reputedly made by the prisoners, too.

By the 9th Duke's tenure (1925-1940), Blackberry Hill was a private nine-hole golf course for family and friends. Aunt Ursie remembers teeing-off above Sligo Gate. Other family stories date back to the Second World War. Nanny Webb, the current Duke's nanny, used to love telling her young charges, especially the boys, the story about a Lancaster bomber that came down on the hill in 1944. Nanny Webb, who at the time was the only resident in the Castle, heard the crash. Jumping on her bike and cycling to the scene, she found an injured airman who had managed to crawl away from the wreckage. She was able to administer first aid to the Rear Gunner before an ambulance arrived but tragically, the rest of the crew had perished. Today, Blackberry Hill is part of our arable farm and the commercial shoot. When I first arrived in 2001, I had to accept that this whole area was for shooting. I can still remember the look of horror on the Beat Keeper's face when, during a ramble, I stumbled across him looking after his birds. I was with a horde of rowdy young children on bikes and ponies.

ABOVE
PHEASANT
Watercolour by Nick Hugh McCann

RIGHT (clockwise from top left)
THE WILD FLOWER, RAGGED ROBIN (*Lychnis flos-cuculi*) which attracts butterflies and bees, thrives on Blackberry Hill

IRONSTONE HAS BEEN QUARRIED all around this beautiful lime tree leaving the roots, still clinging to stone, exposed

THE VIEW FROM BLACKBERRY HILL looking southwest to Church Thorns on the edge of Old Park

Our restoration involved a lot of clearing, as with everywhere else. But the biggest change has been to reinstate Elizabeth's sweet chestnut avenue that had been felled, although no one can remember when or why. We spent months levelling this circuitous route, up to 20 metres wide in places. Decades of neglect had left a thoroughly uneven and overgrown surface. Old 18th-century stone quarry scoops on the edges needed filling in where they had gradually eroded into the avenue. Fillingham had written to the 4th Duke, in December 1785: 'If your Grace prefer Roads being made for the Public, I will also do the best I can, Blackberry Hill Quarry is nearly exhausted, I set the Labourours to try in different places for Stone, but I doubt any proper being found nearer than Woolsthorpe Hill.' Whoever was quarrying had little respect for some of the trees. There is a healthy beech tree on the southwest edge that has clung on to survival despite earth and rock being extracted four or five feet from its base. It illustrates brilliantly how robust tree roots are to keep reaching down for nutrients and water under extreme stress.

OPPOSITE
AUTUMN LEAF CARPET
on Blackberry Hill

RIGHT
ELIZABETH REINSTATED THE AVENUE in about 1804. She planted sweet chestuts alongside Brown's sycamore, lime, beech, oak and London plane. The trees either side of the track are over 250 years old

When the Duke's Walk was being developed, the 5th Duke and Duchess had a lot of fun building grottos along the way. When we were clearing Blackberry Hill towards the Mausoleum, we came across what we thought was a hermitage in the side of a garden wall. As we pulled away more debris it seemed to have more of a significant feel to it than simply an ornamental hermit's dwelling. We had a look in the archives and it turned out to be what King, the 5th Duke's agent, referred to as a, 'Labourer's Cottage on side of Blackberry Hill above Duke's Walk'. It is likely to be the dwelling that was later improved for the watchman in 1829. I never cease to be amazed how many layers of history surface at Belvoir, even in the garden.

ABOVE
THE VIEW OF THE CASTLE from the Mausoleum. Elizabeth had chosen her final resting place long before her sudden death

BELOW
ORNATE WROUGHT-IRON decorates the Mausoleum door

ABOVE
ORIGINAL KEYS engraved 'MAUSOLEUM'

BELOW
THE MAUSOLEUM is surrounded by yew, magnolia and cherry trees. Lady Diana Cooper and her husband, Duff Cooper, are also among those buried here

THE MAUSOLEUM

But perhaps the most significant layer of Belvoir's history, both in the garden and the Castle itself, is wrapped up in the life of Elizabeth. She was behind so much of everything that we live in and look out onto, and one of her favourite views from her bedroom on the southwest front of the Castle looked over the area where she intended her final resting place to be. She marked the spot with silver fir trees.

In a letter to her husband, which she wrote during an earlier illness, she gave strict instructions about where she would like to be buried because she didn't want to finish up with her husband's ancestors five miles away in Bottesford church. 'Dearest of Men – I do not like being poked down at Bottesford I shall like better to be buried in the Middle of Blackberry or Winsor Hill, A plain but Handsome Monument, & Figure in White Marble embracing the two dear Children I have lost.'

LEFT
AN AERIAL VIEW OF THE MAUSOLEUM looking northeast towards the Castle

LEFT
THE MARBLE FIGURE OF ELIZABETH and the children who pre-deceased her, designed by Matthew Cotes Wyatt

OPPOSITE
ON ENTERING THE MAUSEOLUM one is struck by the extraordinary quality of the light illuminating Elizabeth's tomb. At first glance, it would seem to be artificial – in fact, it is sunlight shining through a yellow stained-glass skylight

Elizabeth never saw the plans for her Mausoleum. It fell to the next generation of Wyatts: Benjamin, Philip and Matthew Cotes to build her memorial. They chose a Norman style design in recognition of the family's Norman origins. The plain exterior is contrasted by a theatrical interior which unfolds into contrived spaces with the monumental tomb of Elizabeth at the far end. Matthew Cotes Wyatt designed the tomb with a marble figure of Elizabeth carved in the round, rising towards the cloud-filled heavens with her pre-deceased children reaching out for her – just as she had requested. Lady Diana Cooper described it rather witheringly: 'She floats now in marble in her chapel, surrounded by winged stillborns.'[55] Amazing natural light pours onto the tomb through coloured glass concealed in the roof.

[55] An extract from an article in an American magazine cutting, written in 1984

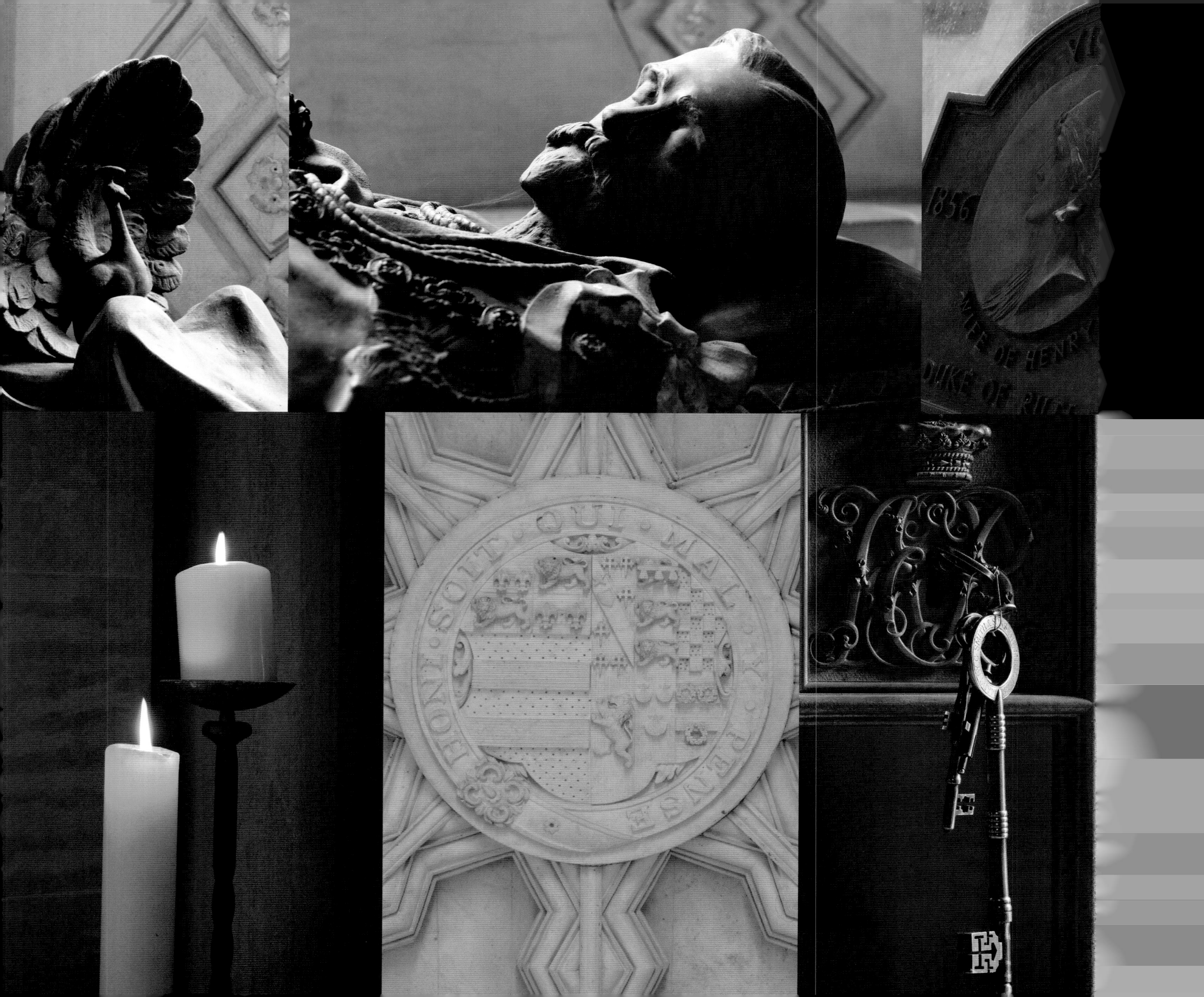
1856
WIFE OF HENRY
HONI SOIT QUI MAL Y PENSE

The Mausoleum's position may have been the spot considered for an obelisk before Brown arrived in 1780. Spyers shows it in line with the ruined St. James's Church in Woolsthorpe that cuts through the 'avenue in Bushy Lady's Close'. The north section of this wood has been taken out and the south section, now called Kennel Wood, gives the appearance that something of significance had always been considered in the place where the building is now.

By 1826, construction had begun and Philip Wyatt was preparing the foundations for Elizabeth's great friend, HRH The Duke of York to lay the foundation stone. Her death left her seven children (the youngest, George, was only five years old) and her husband distraught. HRH and the Duke of Wellington consoled the grieving widower. At the time of her death, HRH, Col Frederick Trench (whose influence and that of his father's in the 4th Duke's day was so pertinent to the finished design of both Castle and garden) and Elizabeth were involved in large-scale building projects in London including a Royal Palace, a new quay on the north bank of the River Thames, a new entrance to Hyde Park Corner and other embellishments in Royal Parks. She was an outstanding woman who took great pride in all her architectural achievements. Mrs Arbuthnott, an acquaintance of Elizabeth's, wrote: 'She certainly was a woman of extraordinary genius and talent mixed up with a great deal of vanity and folly.' She added that Elizabeth, 'had very few female friends, to those few she was most constant and affectionate'.[56]

The Mausoleum was finished in 1827 and the surrounding woodland garden soon after in the same year. Records show that the labourer's cottage was improved in 1829 and the incumbent's job may well have included keeping an eye on the Mausoleum. 'Aged yews' and firs were planted in 1841 and have since been replaced with an avenue of cherry trees.

Since Elizabeth's death, many members of the Manners family have been interred in the building and its grounds. In the late autumn of 2014, we had a big family gathering to plant the woodland garden with bluebells. A party of 20 volunteers from the Loughborough University Students' Association had already spent the day giving us a head start. It was wonderful to spend some time in this most beautiful spot.

After remembering Elizabeth at the Mausoleum, it seems fitting to be ending my tour across what I have come to think of as one of the best monuments to all of Brown's proposals at Belvoir – the astonishing embankment. Its functionality blends so naturally between two steep hillsides that you forget it's entirely manufactured. Brown had planned a perfect Picturesque vista through the woods, across the lakes and up to the ruined church on the far hillside. The view now is still more or less as he intended. Elizabeth added a stream to cascade down the hill to Wyatt's dairy – textbook Picturesque features to add sublime drama. When it was finished it would have been a wonderful example of the two artists' ideas working together.

ABOVE
MAGNOLIA MOLLICOMATA at the rear of the Mausoleum;
NIKKI APPLEWHITE (far right) and the students from Loughborough University, planting bluebells next to the Mausoleum, autumn 2014

OPPOSITE (above)
A MANNERS PEACOCK sits at the foot of the 8th DUKE'S TOMB (centre). **A MEMORIAL PLAQUE** (right) **to the Duke's wife, Violet**

OPPOSITE (below centre)
THE 5th DUKE'S ARMS, paired with the Duchess's Howard family arms and with his Order of the Garter

[56] Francis Bamford and the Duke of Wellington, ed., *The Journal of Mrs Arbuthnot, 1820-1832*, Macmillan, 1950. Mrs Arbuthnot, wife of Charles Arbuthnot MP, was a diarist, social observer and political hostess on behalf of the Tory party. She was a regular visitor to Belvoir, accompanying her husband's great friend the Duke of Wellington and described as his 'closest woman friend.'

To me, the whole landscape is a magical blend of 'old' Brown's magnificent plan for a naturalistic English landscape, with young Elizabeth's spirited and inimitable style. Had she lived beyond 45, the garden (and the Castle) may well have picked up layers of developing tastes, and obscured the remarkable status quo. But, apart from her unfinished projects, very few improvements – bar the necessary – were done at Belvoir after her death. Her husband and later her two sons, the 6th and 7th Dukes, preserved the whole place as a monument to her memory. In 1906, when the 8th Duke returned to run his family home, the place was a relic of another age.

Lady Diana Cooper recalled teenage memories of travelling in the landau, the victoria or the barouche with her grandfather, the 7th Duke, shortly before he died, splashing through the muddy lanes on the Estate. 'When we reached home, a large crowd of tourists would have collected on each side at the last hundred yards of the approach [on the embankment], and my grandfather would uncover his head and bow very slightly with a look of pleasure and welcome on his delicate old face. He loved his tourists. They represented to him England and liberty and the feudal system.' The house and gardens were open to the public three times a week and on all bank holidays, a tradition which the 8th Duke carried on. Diana and her older siblings would be sent off for picnics in the summer to avoid the hordes. As she described it: 'Not that one could get away with one's picnic – they all brought picnics too and were encouraged to eat and sleep and take their boots off and comb their hair in the garden, on the terraces, all about and everywhere. They paid no admittance and two or three elderly ladies in black dresses, Lena the head housemaid...and Mrs Smith the housekeeper, sparkling with jet arabesques, or a pensioned retainer – would shepherd them around.'

It's doubtful that anyone would have mentioned, never mind eulogised about, the Capability Brown landscape. The attractions would have been head gardener Divers' intricately shaped spring flowerbeds and borders on the terraces, as well as Peto's new Rose Garden. Perhaps mention was made about the driving force behind everything they were shown – Elizabeth – and, very likely, the improvements that Violet was working on. The Edwardian era's death duties, along with the effects of the First World War, were a death knell to country estates

like Belvoir. There was no spare cash. Violet managed to make some improvements in 1906, but her husband was forced to sell 13,300 acres in 1920 to pay death duties. To hang on to even part of the Estate, never mind the herbaceous borders, with falling staff numbers and lack of funds, was achievement enough. Most of Divers' beds were grassed over by the time he retired in 1917 and, ironically, the gardens returned to the naturalistic style that Brown had intended.

No one in Britain was creating new Arcadian landscapes, except perhaps for rich bankers or wealthy American heiresses who could afford to maintain old estates or build smaller new ones. While everyone probably recognised Brown's parkland landscapes as the epitome of Englishness, few could remember why or who he was. But in 1927, architectural historian Christopher Hussey acknowledged Brown's positive contribution to English landscape in *The Picturesque: Studies in a Point of View*. It was an influential work that inspired others. Dorothy Stroud's academic study in her book *Capability Brown* published in 1950 is referred to by academics as his definitive biography. It highlighted the enormous extent and scale of his work for the first time. Since then, his popularity has grown and his name has appeared in books, articles and plays. Most notably, Tom Stoppard's play *Arcadia* fabulously sums up the English landscape as being, 'invented by gardeners imitating foreign painters who were evoking classical authors. The whole thing was brought home in the luggage from the grand tour... Capability Brown doing Claude, who was doing Virgil. Arcadia!' But for me, the best source of Brown's work is in the most recent biography *The Omnipotent Magician* by Jane Brown, published in 2011. Not least because you get a feel for what Brown was like as a person, as well as a phenomenal gardener, tirelessly travelling across the country in pursuit of his next challenge; he was amiable, a little bit cheeky and yet thoroughly professional.

OPPOSITE
THE EMBANKMENT on the final approach to the Castle

ABOVE
A BROWNIAN VISTA from the Castle towards Knipton and Croxton Kerrial in the distance

The mounting appreciation of his work brings us neatly to the tercentenary of this great man's birth, in 2016. Historians have seized the opportunity to reevaluate the impact he made on our English scenery and found another 90 gardens attributed to him. Belvoir, once rumoured to have a Brown garden, can now take its rightful place in the prestigious roll call of his 260 parks and gardens. We have restored much of his plan that had been neglected and, like Elizabeth, allowed ourselves the odd contemporary design of our own.

Capability Brown has given every subsequent generation of the Manners family an opportunity to show that they have lived, and it's been a great honour, as well as an enormous responsibility, for us to try to get it right.

BELVOIR TODAY

Today, we manage all of the woodlands sustainably following the UK Woodland Assurance Standard. The volume of timber we harvest each year is less than the annual volume increment, therefore the growing stock is increasing. We maintain a very good carbon footprint – the Castle is heated using wood chips from timber grown on the Estate – and we also sell firewood throughout the Vale of Belvoir.

We follow management guidelines as set out in the Forestry Commission (FC) 'Forests and Biodiversity' guidelines. These cover the following:

Priority habitats and species: These are managed according to the FC Woodland Birds Project for threatened native woodland species.
Native woodlands: Native trees, mostly oak, are planted when re-stocking felled woodland.
Landscape ecology: We provide linkages between associated habitats such as grassland and water bodies.
Ecological processes: A diverse woodland structure benefits many species.
Native trees and shrubs: Species are selected which will perform well on the site and provide genetic diversity.
Forest and stand structure: Structural diversity creates a range of habitats.
Veteran trees and deadwood: Both standing and fallen dead wood is retained; old trees are particularly significant for woodland diversity.
Open, scrub and edge habitats: These are managed to provide important resources and habitats for biodiversity.
Riparian zones: We protect riparian systems and linear habitat linkages.
Invasive species: These are controlled, especially non-native species such as rhododendron.
Grazing and browsing: Livestock are fenced out of woodland and non-native deer are controlled to protect and enhance biodiversity.

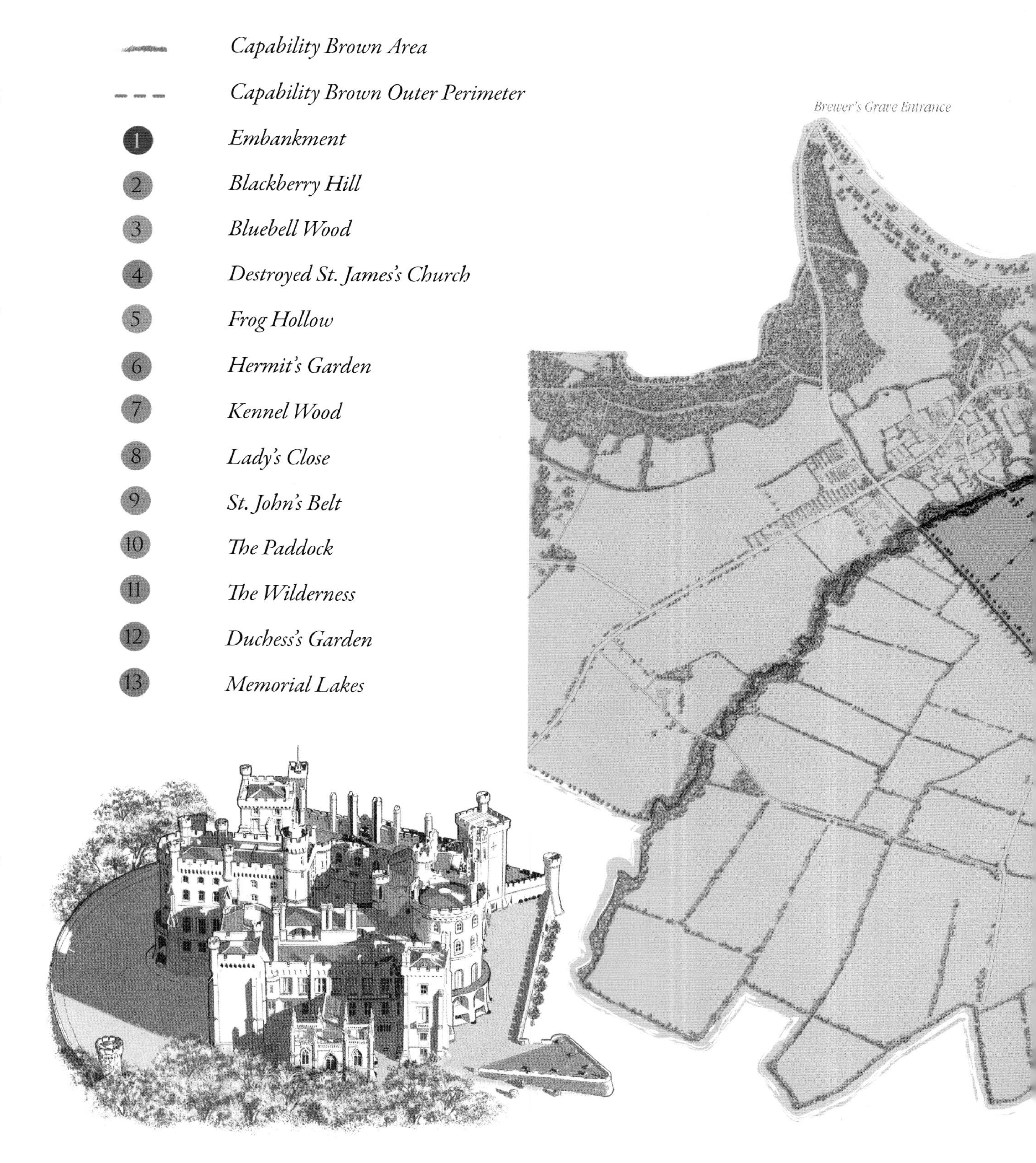

Capability Brown Area
Cricket Ground
13
Memorial Lakes
4
Destroyed St. James's Church
Devon Park
King's Wood
Woolsthorpe Park
Knipton Pasture
Granby Wood
thorpe Village
7
Kennel Wood
5
Frog Hollow
8
Lady's Close
Windsor Hill
2
Blackberry Hill
Capability Brown Outer Perimeter
N
10
The Paddock
Hermit's Garden
6
Capability Brown Area
9
St. John's Belt
12
Duchess's Garden
11
The Wilderness
Sligo Gate
High Leys
Bluebell Wood
3
1
Embankment
Old Park Wood
Church Thorns
The Ash Beds
The Bushes
Saltbecks
0
125
250
500
750
1,000
Meters

INDEX

AUTHOR'S ACKNOWLEDGEMENTS

THE DUCHESS OF RUTLAND

When we started restoring Capability Brown's landscape at Belvoir we didn't realise just how enormous the task was going to be. Long gone are the days when the Estate employed up to 50 gardeners. Today, the job is contracted out to Applewhite Garden Design Ltd, a fantastic and innovative horticultural team headed by Nikki Applewhite and Martin Gibbs. We simply couldn't have achieved all that we have in the gardens without their expertise and amazing hard work. I also owe a special thanks to all the many volunteers Nikki recruits for their incredibly skilled contributions to the maintenance of the terraces and woodland gardens.

Everything we do in the landscape has to fit in with our commercial shoot. Capability Brown was as mindful about cover drives in the 18th century as we have to be here today, and much of the framework is already in place. Our agent, Phil Burtt, has been a constant source of support. As well as being shoot captain, he has a wonderful eye for landscape design, and is the strength and action man behind all my requests.

Our woodland gardens owe a special debt of gratitude to Charles Williams of Burncoose Nurseries. Since meeting him at Chelsea Flower Show in 2003 he has become a great business partner and friend, and his own magnificent woodland gardens at Caerhays Castle have provided a continuous source of inspiration to me. A very special thanks, too, to Richard Sochacki, our forester, who has supervised the thinning and replanting of the huge acreage of trees that make up Brown's perimeter tree belt, avenues and clumps of trees.

Steffie Shields was the first Capability Brown expert I met in 2008 to help us understand the significance of our landscape, and her beautiful words about the garden have been extremely useful in this book. The history has been brought to life through John Phibb's incredibly in-depth research. His enthusiasm for Capability Brown and his work to celebrate the tercentenary of his birth has been the focus of our restoration project. Together with our archivist, Peter Foden, we have discovered the secrets behind many of the decisions made in the past that have helped us to prioritise work today.

A special thanks to Alan Titchmarsh, who I have met on numerous occasions and had the privilege of working with on a recent television programme, for finding the time in his busy schedule to write our foreword. Thanks to Martin Reeves for his stunning aerial photography. Andy Bates for his superb interpretation of countless aerial shots and old surveys for his illustrated map. To our brilliant editor, Eloise Manners who gave us great help with the book's structure as well as giving the book its polish with her invaluable skills. And to Nick Hugh McCann, who having photographed most of the pictures in my first book *Belvoir Castle – 1000 years of History, Art and Architecture*, has risen to the challenge again and taken the truly spectacular shots for this one, too. He has also put the whole book together with his huge artistic flair for page design.

And finally, my thanks to Jane Pruden who, as always, has put my thoughts into words and steered the whole book from concept to finish. Both of us would like to thank Katie Bates for all her support in my office, and John Phibbs, Nikki Applewhite, Martin Gibbs, Charles Williams, Peter Foden, Richard Sochacki, Caroline Stewart, Emma Ellis and Sarah Davison for reading the manuscript and making necessary corrections.

CAPABILITY BROWN & BELVOIR

DISCOVERING A LOST LANDSCAPE

Additional photographs:
Gary Hope (pp10, 80, 115, 145, 221); Brian Moody (p129); Martin Neeves (pp17, 63, 66, 119, 134, 153, 174-5, 194, 201);
Karol Pawlak (p120); Skyscan (p207)

Map of Belvoir today by Andrew Bates, Bates Fine Art-Design Limited, www.batesfineart.com

Photography and book design by
Nick Hugh McCann BA
Published by Nick McCann Associates Ltd 2015
www.nickhughmccann.com

ISBN 978-0-9516891-6-5

THE FIRST LAWNMOWER, 1830
Budding's Patent. N3157

Dorling Kindersley / UIG / Bridgeman

L Brown

CAPABILITY BROWN & BELVOIR

DISCOVERING A LOST LANDSCAPE

The Duchess of Rutland with Jane Pruden
Photography and book design by Nick Hugh McCann

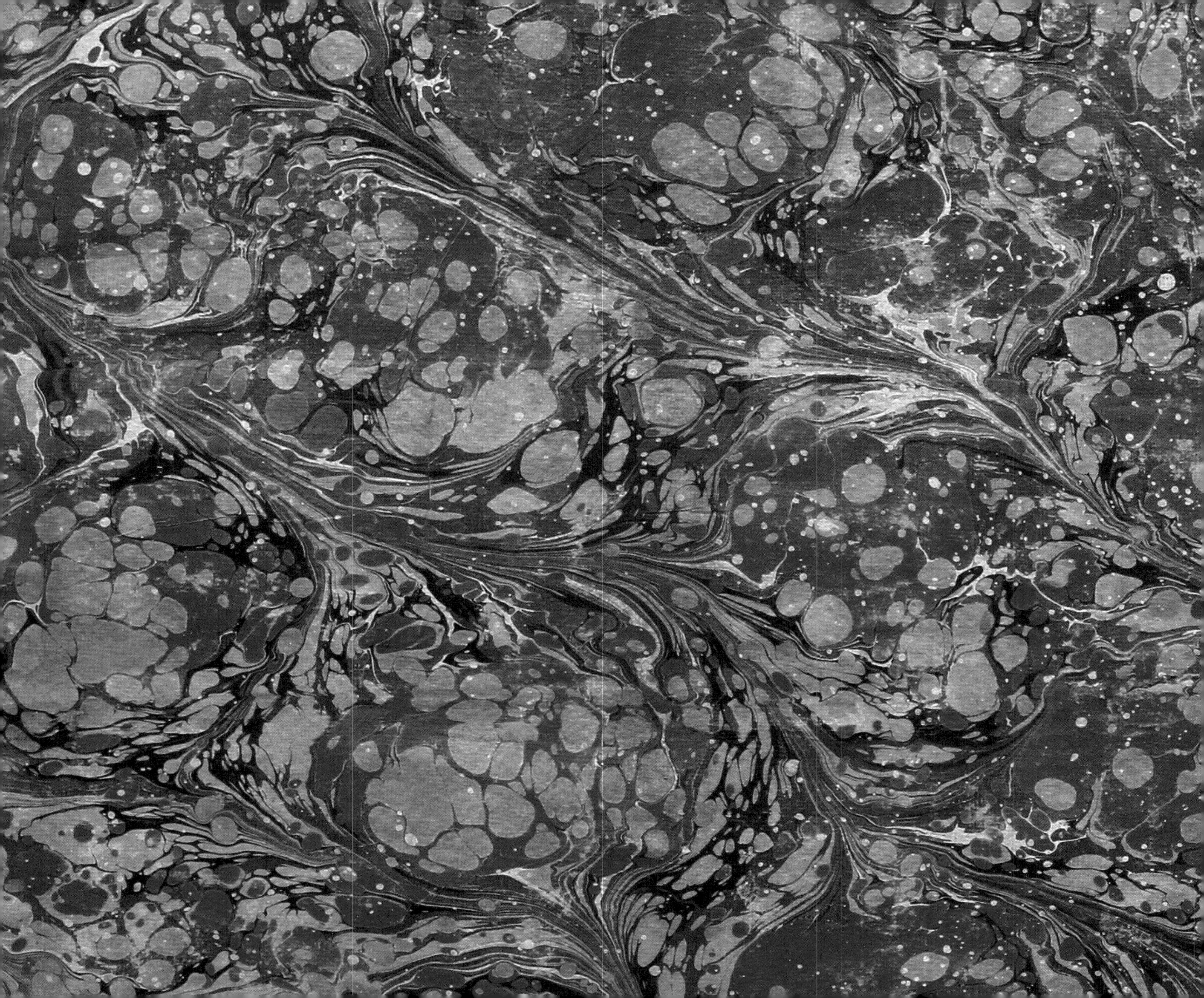